Cambridge Elements ≡

Elements in Economics of Emerging Markets
edited by
Bruno S. Sergi
Harvard University

DIGITALIZATION IN EMERGING ECONOMIES

Mark Esposito
*Hult International Business School and
Berkman Klein Center for Internet and Society
at Harvard University*

Yusaf Akbar
Central European University

Francis Xavier Campbell
Central European University

CAMBRIDGE
UNIVERSITY PRESS

Shaftesbury Road, Cambridge CB2 8EA, United Kingdom

One Liberty Plaza, 20th Floor, New York, NY 10006, USA

477 Williamstown Road, Port Melbourne, VIC 3207, Australia

314–321, 3rd Floor, Plot 3, Splendor Forum, Jasola District Centre,
New Delhi – 110025, India

103 Penang Road, #05–06/07, Visioncrest Commercial, Singapore 238467

Cambridge University Press is part of Cambridge University Press & Assessment,
a department of the University of Cambridge.

We share the University's mission to contribute to society through the pursuit of
education, learning and research at the highest international levels of excellence.

www.cambridge.org
Information on this title: www.cambridge.org/9781009598750

DOI: 10.1017/9781009433921

When citing this work, please include a reference to the DOI 10.1017/9781009433921

First published 2025

A catalogue record for this publication is available from the British Library

ISBN 978-1-009-59875-0 Hardback
ISBN 978-1-009-43390-7 Paperback
ISSN 2631-8598 (online)
ISSN 2631-858X (print)

Digitalization in Emerging Economies

Elements in Economics of Emerging Markets

DOI: 10.1017/9781009433921
First published online: February 2025

Mark Esposito
*Hult International Business School and Berkman Klein Center
for Internet and Society at Harvard University*

Yusaf Akbar
Central European University

Francis Xavier Campbell
Central European University

Author for correspondence: Mark Esposito, mark.esposito@faculty.hult.edu

Abstract: *Digitalization in Emerging Economies* offers a comprehensive exploration of digitalization's transformative potential in the Global South. The Element examines the digital revolution's impact on businesses, governments, and individuals in emerging economies. It highlights the paradigm shift in these markets due to advancements like mobile technology, internet connectivity, e-commerce platforms, and digital payment systems. The Element also addresses challenges such as privacy, cybersecurity, and the digital divide. It explores the drivers and barriers of digital adoption, the effects on industries and labor markets, and the role of government policies in shaping digital ecosystems. *Digitalization in Emerging Economies* aims to guide those navigating the digital landscape in a rapidly changing world, contributing to the discourse on leveraging digital technologies for inclusive and sustainable development.

This Element also has a video abstract: Cambridge.org/EEM_Esposito

Keywords: digitization, emerging economies, tech innovation, socioeconomic development, digital policy

ISBNs: 9781009598750 (HB), 9781009433907 (PB), 9781009433921 (OC)
ISSNs: 2631-8598 (online), 2631-858X (print)

Contents

1 Introduction

In an era marked by rapid technological advancement and globalization, the digitalization of emerging markets has the potential to be a transformative event in world economic history by reshaping the economies, societies, and livelihoods in the Global South (Mustaf et al., 2020). Increasing digital interconnectedness in emerging markets presents both opportunities and challenges for the public and private sectors in the context of innovation, development, and inclusion. The core purpose of this Element is to delve into this multifaceted landscape, exploring its dynamics, implications, and potential for fostering sustainable growth and equitable progress.

There is no single official definition or classification of what constitutes an emerging market economy, with many authors and organizations having proposed different definitions and classification systems over the years. Throughout this Element, we use the terms "emerging economies," "emerging markets," and "emerging market economies" interchangeably and explore the multitude of these definitions to synthesize their unique points into a more holistic picture of what emerging economies are and can be. In general, we follow the broad definition proposed by Green Templeton College (n.d.) that emerging market economies are those that have made significant strides toward political, social, and economic progress in recent years but still face systemic issues with political instability and less developed and reliable systems and institutions. Examples of emerging market economies include India, China, Mexico, Russia, Turkey, Brazil, and other nations in regions such as the Middle East, Africa, and Southeast Asia.

Recent digitalization in emerging markets represents a paradigm shift in how businesses operate, governments govern, and individuals interact (Karpenko et al., 2023). In this Element, we use the term "digitalization" interchangeably with "digital transformation," which is defined as "a process of adoption of digital tools and methods by an organization, typically those that have either not been including the digital factor as part of their core activities or have not kept up with the pace of change in digital technologies" (Observatory of Public Sector Innovation, n.d., para. 1)." The adoption of digital tools and methods extends beyond individual organizations to the use of digital technologies in trade, economic relations, and political practices (Petlach, 2023).

This phenomenon represents a paradigm shift in emerging economies because it fundamentally changes economic and social relations and governance processes. From the proliferation of mobile technology and internet connectivity to the rise of e-commerce platforms and digital payment systems, the digital revolution fundamentally alters emerging economies' economic and social fabric (Cendrello & Bertrand, 2022). Whereas citizens' economic and social participation was once limited to their immediate surroundings, now they have access to information, commerce, and communication that transcends the boundaries of geography. Businesses and governments have a chance to increase their competitiveness and cultivate a presence on the world economic stage. The rise of digital governance, which refers to the process of embedding digital technology into processes and structures of governance (Engvall & Flak, 2022), is providing a solid foundation for emerging economies to accelerate their development.

Moreover, much of this digitalization differs from its historical counterpart in the developed world in that its growth and diffusion have exploited disruptive, low-cost digital solutions intimately dependent on mobile and wireless technologies (Allmann & Radu, 2023). Nevertheless, amidst the promises of greater efficiency, connectivity, and empowerment, digitalization also brings forth complex issues related to privacy, cybersecurity, and the digital divide, the latter of which refers to "the distinction between those who have access to the internet or other digital technologies and are able to make use of online services, and those who are excluded from these services" (Eurostat, n.d., para. 1). These considerations pose profound challenges to policymakers, businesses, and society.

Drawing on a combination of theoretical frameworks and empirical research, this Element comprehensively examines digitalization in emerging markets from an explicitly multi-disciplinary perspective. It explores the drivers and barriers of digital adoption, the impact of digital technologies on industries and labor markets, and the role of government policies in shaping digital ecosystems. Moreover, it examines the sociocultural dynamics of digitalization, including its implications for identity, inequality, and social inclusion.

By shedding light on the opportunities and pitfalls of digitalization in emerging markets, this Element aims to inform policymakers, practitioners, scholars, and students about the complexities of navigating the digital landscape in a rapidly changing world. It seeks to contribute to the ongoing discourse on harnessing digital technologies for inclusive and sustainable development in emerging economies through nuanced analysis and actionable insights. What follows is a nuanced summary of the primary elements of the first four sections of this manuscript.

Section 2 examines challenges and roadblocks to digitalization in a broad and generalizable context. Section 3 introduces the specifics of emerging markets and how this shapes digitalization processes. Section 4 offers readers specific models and strategies for e-government. It identifies fundamental principles of e-government, a "by-design" framework for e-government and examines e-government initiatives and strategies in a series of emerging economies. Section 5 explores the key dimensions of digitization of Government Services focusing on three complementary and potentially contradictory elements: accountability, efficiency, and democracy. The section argues that successful digitization is not a one-off but a long and multifaceted process requiring considerable attention for governments. Section 6 is a concluding section that summarizes key findings and a broad policy agenda for advancing digitalization initiatives in emerging economies with the aim of securing the efficient and effective implementation and widespread adoption of digital technologies. The goal of this agenda is to enable a sustainable and inclusive digital economy driven by innovation.

Section 2 argues that digital transformation allows governments worldwide to enhance innovation, streamline processes, and promote equity. While developed nations have made significant strides, emerging economies encounter challenges, including resource constraints and sociocultural and political factors (Kauma et al., 2022). This section delves into these challenges, highlighting differences between developed and emerging economies and offering best practices to overcome them.

Digital transformation, or digitalization, involves integrating digital tools and methods into public sector operations, facilitating data-driven decision-making, and improving citizen services (Organisation for Economic Co-operation and Development [OECD], 2021). While this principle is relevant in theory for emerging economies, this process faces numerous hurdles in emerging economies. These barriers include financial limitations in the regulatory framework and availability of financial resources to build digital infrastructure, inadequate broader economic infrastructure, and sociocultural and political barriers that resist adopting digital technology (Kauma et al., 2022).

Offering public services via advanced digital platforms, making digital services accessible to remote and rural areas, and providing underserved areas with high-speed internet connectivity can all increase the reach and effectiveness of digitalization efforts (Allmann & Radu, 2023). Innovation can be enabled by enacting policies that promote and protect digital business models, with protections for electronic transactions and personal data, balancing the needs of businesses with those of consumers. International trade and collaboration can also be supported by developing a regulatory environment that allows for the secure flow of data across national borders (Hammerschmid et al., 2023).

Diving deeper into sociocultural challenges, the section identifies linguistic diversity, cultural resistance, and low digital literacy among the population (relative to more developed countries). For example, access to platforms in multiple languages is crucial, particularly in regions with numerous ethnic and tribal societies. Furthermore, cultural resistance to technology adoption, especially in rural areas, necessitates tailored approaches and significant investments in community engagement (Yavwa & Twinomurinzi, 2021). Lastly, addressing gender disparities in digital literacy requires targeted educational initiatives and outreach efforts in emerging economies.

Section 2 also addresses digitalization's political challenges in emerging economies, including corruption and instability. As with all public investment, the prevalence of corruption risks diverting funds meant for digital projects, which is worsened by the presence of bureaucratic inefficiencies that further delay progress. Political instability disrupts projects and deters investment, particularly in authoritarian regimes where transparency and accountability may be lacking (Mustaf et al., 2020). Authoritarian governments may resist digitalization due to its potential to increase transparency and accountability, posing additional challenges (Huang & Tsai, 2022).

Section 2 then reflects on how these challenges can be overcome. A multifaceted approach is essential to address the sociocultural and political roadblocks. Community engagement, research, and collaboration are key to addressing sociocultural challenges and ensuring inclusivity (Gupta, 2023). In navigating political hurdles, emphasizing short-term wins, collaborating with international partners, and promoting interdepartmental coordination are essential and effective strategies. Establishing centralized governance bodies and adhering to digital standards and cybersecurity protocols are essential for project success (Koop & Kessler, 2021).

The section concludes that while emerging economies face formidable challenges in digital transformation, proactive strategies can surmount these barriers. Through a careful and nuanced understanding of cultural issues, fostering collaboration, and navigating political complexities, these nations can harness the transformative power of digitalization to drive economic and social progress (Yavwa & Twinomurinzi, 2021).

Section 3 delves into the salience of emerging market contexts in both organizational development and policymaking, particularly in the realm of digitalization, with an emphasis on the impact of the emerging market socioeconomic environment on policy practices. In particular, the section explores how digitalization unfolds differently in emerging market contexts compared to developed economies due primarily to distinct institutional landscapes.

Emerging markets, characterized by rapid growth and transitioning from low- to middle-income status, exhibit standard features such as faster economic growth rates, rapid urbanization, abundant natural resources, youthful demographics, and the need for significant infrastructure development (Mustaf et al., 2020). However, considerable heterogeneity exists across these markets, influenced by factors like demographics, geopolitics, and levels of democra-tization. Recognizing this diversity is essential in designing digitalization agendas in emerging economies (Onsongo, 2023).

Institutional theory plays a crucial role in understanding emerging markets, with institutional voids representing unique structural weaknesses. These voids, ranging from legal and regulatory inconsistencies to inadequate financial infra-structure, pose challenges for businesses and investors operating in emerging markets, influencing entry barriers and investment decisions (Kauma et al., 2022). Despite these challenges, digitalization presents opportunities for eco-nomic development in emerging markets, particularly in the public sector. Public sector digitalization initiatives aim to enhance efficiency, transparency, innovation, service accessibility, infrastructure development, data-driven deci-sion-making, and global competitiveness (OECD, 2023).

However, challenges such as limited digital infrastructure access, disparities in digital literacy, cybersecurity risks, and lack of reliable data protection frameworks need to be addressed (Onsongo, 2023). To overcome these chal-lenges, emerging markets can leverage technology leapfrogging, adopting advanced digital technologies to bypass traditional developmental stages. Section 3 proposes various public sector digitalization initiatives, including e-government portals, digital identity systems, mobile government services, e-education, e-healthcare, smart agriculture, digital finance infrastructure, smart city initiatives, and e-procurement systems. These initiatives contribute to more efficient governance, improved service delivery, and enhanced socioeconomic development in emerging markets.

In conclusion, the section advocates for emerging market governments to embrace digital technology leapfrogging to overcome institutional voids and accelerate public sector digitalization efforts. Comparative analysis in Section 4 further explores best practices in e-government design for emerging markets, providing insights for policymakers and practitioners in navigating the complex landscape of digitalization in these contexts.

Section 4 explores the principles, criteria, and cultural factors essential for successful e-government initiatives and a comparative analysis of countries implementing e-government projects. The section considers "by design" prin-ciples that emphasize leveraging digital technology to enhance government services, focusing on digital privacy, openness, and automation. These prin-ciples are developed and deployed to ensure user-centric, secure, and efficient e-government systems (OECD, 2021). The section describes key e-government criteria that should feature in the design of e-government initiatives. These include accessibility, user-centric design, security, interoperability, electronic payments, transparency, efficiency, digital identity, inclusion, cross-agency collaboration, legal framework, scalability, and feedback mechanisms. These criteria serve as the critical signposts necessary for the successful development of digitalization of government services.

The section moves on to case studies of successful e-government projects. Successful e-government implementations cross-nationally in Estonia, India, Rwanda, South Korea, the UAE, and Uruguay demonstrate digital innovation's salient role, robust legal frameworks, and citizen trust. In concrete terms, these countries offer various services that serve as pillars of a functioning e-government, such as unique digital IDs for every citizen, authentication, centralized portals, health, education, justice, and smart city initiatives.

Section 4 then explores some dangers and barriers to e-government. There are many barriers, risks, and roadblocks to implementing e-government in emerging economies, although the technology holds vast potential for improving public services, encouraging transparency, and improving governance processes via digital systems and tools. Risk management is thus crucial for e-government, involving cybersecurity measures, data encryption, access control, privacy compliance, audits, incident response, user education, and continuous improvement (OECD, 2021). Moreover, organizational and bureaucratic culture significantly influence e-government development. Many of the basic tenets of e-government, such as replacing physical paper trails with digital databases, run against decades (if not centuries) of bureaucratic traditions and legal notions of proof and authenticity.

The section then looks at current and emerging trends in e-Government, specifically with regards to Blockchain, Artificial Intelligence (AI), and Quantum Computing. Each of which is pivotal and key for the future of e-Government, Blockchain through enhancing security, transparency and efficiency in transactions and records, AI enhances decision making and better identification and mitigation of risks, and Quantum Computing holds promise for improved e-government through faster and larger data processing via Big Data Analytics and complex modeling which enables simulations for socioeconomic and environmental issues. Quantum Encryption is also helpful for creating unbreakable security for communication and transactions and expands cybersecurity through advanced pattern analysis.

Section 4 concludes with case studies illustrating how vital it remains that government cultures fostering innovation, customer-centricity, collaboration, transparency, data-driven decision-making, change management, leadership, digital literacy, flexibility, ethical considerations, and adaptability are all essential for successful e-government initiatives.

Section 5 explores the key dimensions of digitization of government services focusing on three complementary and potentially contradictory elements: accountability, efficiency, and democracy. While emerging economies are increasingly adopting digital government services, which significantly contribute to economic growth, enhance citizen inclusion, and improve global competitiveness, a lack of proper oversight and strategic planning can endanger these digitalization efforts and risks reinforcing existing inefficiencies, corruption, and authoritarian practices. To avoid these pitfalls, Section 5 asserts that governments must develop and implement comprehensive regulatory frameworks tailored to their specific needs and circumstances. These frameworks should have the following characteristics.

Robust regulatory frameworks are essential for governing the digitization of public services. Given the complexities of digital technologies, these frameworks must ensure effective communication and collaboration across multiple government agencies and external stakeholders. Additionally, governments should engage with international regulatory bodies and think tanks to stay informed on the latest risks and benefits of digital innovations. Collaboration across public, private, and third sectors can further enhance these efforts.

One key regulatory focus should be data protection, emphasizing citizens' data rights, the responsibilities of data handlers, and limits on the use of personal data for commercial or surveillance purposes. Clear enforcement mechanisms are crucial, as they deter misuse and ensure accountability. While governments can draw inspiration from frameworks like the EU's GDPR, they must adapt these regulations to their local cultural, social, and political contexts rather than imposing foreign models wholesale.

In addition to regulations, e-government platforms should prioritize data privacy and security. Developers must collect only essential data, use encryption to protect it, and offer citizens transparency about how their data will be used. Cybersecurity is also a critical concern, and governments should create national cybersecurity strategies, conduct regular audits, and develop crisis management plans. International partnerships can help emerging economies strengthen their cybersecurity infrastructure.

Finally, public awareness and digital literacy are key to the success of these initiatives. Governments should invest in outreach campaigns and training sessions to educate citizens on the benefits of digital services. Engaging with the public at the grassroots level, through schools, community centers, and local councils, can also provide valuable feedback to ensure these services meet citizens' needs.

Section 6 is a concluding section that summarizes the main arguments of the Element and offers key policy recommendations for digital transformation in emerging economies.

Moving Forward

Ultimately, successful digitalization in emerging economies requires a holistic approach, involving regulation, technology, and civic engagement. With the right strategies, these economies can foster sustainable growth and emerge as global leaders in digital governance.

Digital transformation can significantly enhance the economic growth of emerging economies, and this Element aims to investigate this crucial juncture in these nations' societal and economic development. Nevertheless, digital transformation is not an easy endeavor, even for developed economies, and emerging economies face numerous hurdles to implementing digital technologies and initiatives. A lack of digital and internet infrastructure, especially in rural areas, remains a persistent hurdle, which prevents the implementation of more advanced digital systems such as digital payment systems (Onsongo, 2023). Digital skills are also often lacking among citizens in emerging economies, with digital literacy initiatives needed to help citizens build their digital and technical capabilities in order to be able to use digital services (Yavwa & Twinomurinzi, 2021).

Finances and funding are another roadblock to successful digitalization initiatives, with public and private sector organizations struggling with the same financial barriers. Digital infrastructure has a high cost and requires a significant investment in time and resources, which is not always readily at the disposal of public and private sector organizations in emerging economies (Cendrello & Bertrand, 2022). Regulatory frameworks also tend to be underdeveloped or lack a specific focus on digitalization and emerging technologies, such as AI, hindering the rate at which these technologies can be developed and deployed without facing ethical and legal concerns, such as data protection and privacy. In emerging economies, traditional social structures, economic practices, and cultural norms can leave citizens resistant to uptake digital technologies that will change the way they do business and conduct their everyday lives (Wandaogo, 2022). This resistance to change is a more complex hurdle that still needs to be overcome if digitalization initiatives are to be successful.

The financial burden of funding digitalization projects can be overcome if private and public sector organizations pool their resources through private–public partnerships (PPPs), which are established methods for funding welfare projects and other public initiatives in emerging economies (World Economic Forum & FTI Consulting, 2023). The digital divide can be bridged in these economies by putting together targeted efforts and projects to reach digitally disadvantaged populations while being sensitive to their unique cultural identity and economic and social needs (Gupta, 2023). Digital technology can become a catalyst for inclusive, sustainable development, spearheaded by strategic and proactive approaches on the part of governments and their private partners. Digitalization also has great potential to revolutionize supply chains, energy management, agriculture, and other areas of sustainability beyond public sector and government functions, which goes to show how crucial it is for governments to take the first step in establishing digital infrastructure and services.

Finally, digital transformation across emerging economies must be grounded in social impact and added value for citizens' daily lives. Belief in social impact requires trust in governments to use digital technology to address social challenges, from healthcare access to education quality, aiming for broad societal benefits (Koop & Kessler, 2021). Citizens will have more trust in such government strategies if they engage in international forums to align with global standards and practices for digital trade, interoperability, and technology collaboration. Citizens need to see their governments participate in knowledge and expertise exchange programs with other nations to learn from global best practices in digitalization.

Implementing this policy agenda requires trust from citizens, who are often cynical about digital transformation as a means for corrupt and unstable governments to pursue funding for the benefit of the few at the top of the economic pyramid (OECD, 2023). We believe citizens' trust can be built through sustained, coordinated efforts across government, the private sector, civil society, and international partners. These efforts include continuous evaluation, improvement, and adaptation to technological advancements and societal needs, ensuring that digitalization initiatives remain relevant and effective in driving growth and development in emerging economies (Asian Productivity Organization [APO], 2021).

Despite these challenges, this Element's authors remain optimistic about enacting digital transformation in emerging countries through proactive strategies and actions that can help emerging economies overcome barriers and harness the benefits of digital transformation. Governments must prioritize investments in digital infrastructure to ensure widespread and affordable internet access and digital services and implement extensive educational and training programs to improve digital literacy and skills among the workforce (Onsongo, 2023). Funding, mentorship, and policies create a supportive ecosystem for startups and innovators. Establishing regulatory sandboxes to allow startups and businesses to test innovative digital and financial products in a controlled environment can ensure consumer protection (Ciancarini et al., 2024). To ensure consumer protection, emerging economies must develop feasible national cybersecurity strategies to protect critical infrastructure, businesses, and citizens' privacy. Moreover, citizens' privacy can be further expanded through digital identities, and communities can be educated to trust user-friendly digital identity systems that respect privacy and enhance access to digital services (OECD, 2021).

The Global South can transform its citizens' livelihoods and social and economic prospects by driving forward digitalization initiatives. With growing access to healthcare and education, increasing economic growth, and more accessible, inclusive and efficient public services and governance, these regions can leap forward in social and economic development. Global markets can be enhanced by the presence of entrepreneurs and small businesses who previously would not have been able to access the global market, driving forth job creation and innovation (Cendrello & Bertrand, 2022). A more inclusive global economy can be fostered through the digitalization of emerging markets, which will see a boost in equity, productivity, and sustainability, creating a more inclusive global economy and allowing these markets to compete with equal prospects on the world stage.

2 Challenges and Roadblocks to Digitalization in Emerging Economies

Introduction

Digital transformation poses a rich opportunity for governments around the world to drive forward innovation in public sector functions, streamline previously cumbersome and inefficient processes and services, and open up the paths for more equity and inclusion for all citizens in society (EMnet Working Group on Digital Transformation in Emerging Markets [EWGDTEM], 2022). There has been a significant investment in digitalization in governments around the world. The 2022 United Nations E-Government Development Index indicates that the scores for most UN countries have risen since the COVID-19 pandemic, with two-thirds of the world's nations now having "High" or "Very High" scores (United Nations Department of Economic and Social Affairs [UNDESA], 2022). Emerging economies lag behind developed nations in such efforts, but their growth has been notable in recent years – African countries, for example, have moved upward in the index faster than any other region since 2016 (UNDESA, 2022).

Emerging economies face unique challenges when implementing digitalization in the public sector. Resources and infrastructure remain persistent hurdles, especially in digitalizing government services (Mustaf et al., 2020). Beyond finances and infrastructure, however, sociocultural and political factors remain another substantial roadblock to implementing public sector digital transformation (Organisation for Economic Co-operation and Development [OECD],

2021). This section explores the sociocultural and political challenges and roadblocks to implementing digitalization in the public sector in emerging economies. We first define digital transformation (which we use interchangeably with "digitalization" in this section) and provide an overview of the characteristics and principles of this phenomenon in the public sector. We then explore digitalization in the public sector in emerging economies, focusing on sociocultural and political challenges and roadblocks and identifying significant differences between developed nations and emerging economies. We conclude with best practices for overcoming these roadblocks and increasing the success of digitalization efforts and strategies.

Characteristics and Principles of Digital Transformation in the Public Sector

Digital transformation has been defined as "a process of adoption of digital tools and methods by an organization, typically those that have either not been including the digital factor as part of their core activities or have not kept up with the pace of change in digital technologies" (Observatory of Public Sector Innovation, n.d., para. 1). Digital transformation involves implementing digital technologies and processes into the functions and operations of a public sector organization, including its primary business operations, how it interacts with citizens and provides services, and how it gathers public information to be used for government uses (Cendrello & Bertrand, 2022). This process is often disruptive and iterative and challenges the traditional status quo of public sector organizations (Halkias et al., 2023; Tse et al., 2023).

Digital transformation fundamentally involves integrating big data and data-driven decision-making into the organization. Decisions that were once made via one or more human actors or cumbersome analogue processes are now streamlined into an empirical, evidence-based process (Edelmann et al., 2023). Vast amounts of data are gathered and analyzed to enhance the delivery of services, inform policy-making and other decisions, and analyze the results of operations processes (Edelmann et al., 2023). The data is gathered from various sources, such as publicly available datasets and records, Internet of Things devices, online services, processes, and interactions (Esposito & Kapoor, 2022). Data-driven decision-making also involves using advanced analytics and AI (machine learning, data mining, predictive analytics, etc.) to analyze the data and draw conclusions by identifying trends and patterns (Esposito & Kapoor, 2022).

Beyond just the powers and risks of advanced technologies, digitalization also poses an excellent opportunity to make public sector operations and citizen services more user-friendly and human-centric (Trischler & Westman Trischler, 2022). The process of accessing public services has long been known to be slow, inefficient, bureaucratic, corrupt, and under-resourced. Digitizing these processes shifts the focus from traditional governance processes to center on citizens' preferences, needs, and considerations (OECD, 2021). Digital technologies, especially in the realm of e-government, can make citizen services faster, more efficient, and more accessible, which can enhance citizens' satisfaction with and trust in government (Enaifoghe et al., 2023). E-government platforms have been pushing forward innovations in personalized services, such as offering personalized healthcare or tax information based on a citizen's profile and any publicly available information about them (Enaifoghe et al., 2023).

Despite digital transformation's positive potential, it must be centered around certain principles to ensure digitalization initiatives are executed correctly and sustained beyond an initial hype period (Esposito & Kapoor, 2022). The most crucial core principles are transparency, accountability, agility, and human resources. Transparency and accountability are core tenets of effective digital public sector projects (Mynenko & Lyulyov, 2022). The integration of digital tools, platforms, and processes into the public sector is often accompanied by the aim to make governance more transparent and public authorities more accountable, with traceable exchanges and transactions enabled by data analytics, Internet of Things devices, blockchain, and the like (Valle-Cruz & García-Contreras, 2023).

An agile approach to governance, combined with an innovative and collaborative mindset, is also crucial to the success of digitalization projects. In this sense, agility refers to the ability of the public sector to respond adaptively to new technologies, social trends, and citizen needs (Looks, 2022). Services, processes, and strategies need to be adjusted in response to feedback, trends, and regulations, a holistic, iterative, and constantly ongoing process rather than linear and fixed (Abdullah et al., 2023). In terms of digital initiatives, this process involves developing, piloting, and deploying initiatives in small increments, regularly soliciting feedback from experts and the public, and adjusting the initiative along the way (Ciancarini et al., 2024).

An innovation mindset is crucial to effective agility because it allows experimentation and calculated risk-taking needed to develop technologies and platforms that genuinely address public needs (Asian Productivity Organization, 2021). Collaboration and knowledge-sharing enhance the innovation capacities of the public sector. Collaboration can include partnerships between public sector entities, such as public healthcare, public universities, citizen services centers, and public welfare offices (Hammerschmid et al., 2023). Nevertheless, even richer results can be achieved when the public sector collaborates with other sectors of society, such as private-sector companies, academic institutions, international organizations, and third-sector charities (World Economic Forum & FTI Consulting, 2023).

Finally, amid the race toward newer and better technologies and more creative and profound innovations, the value of human resources in the digital transformation process cannot be underestimated. First, developing digital platforms and digitizing public processes requires a digitally literate workforce with the right skills, training, and certifications (Esposito & Kapoor, 2022). Reskilling and upskilling initiatives in digital literacy, data analytics, and emerging technologies for public sector employees are crucial to achieving higher levels of digital literacy (Kitsios et al., 2023). Training in agile methodologies for project management will also prove beneficial for building an agile governance mindset (Kaczorowska, 2020). Finally, the end users of the platforms, processes, or services in question also need to have an adequate level of digital literacy to utilize them efficiently. Achieving this level of digital literacy in the public can prove to be a longer-term project that may involve integrating greater digital literacy education into the education system, developing informative communications campaigns about the new digital platforms and processes, and facilitating training to the public through local governance and outreach initiatives (Allmann & Radu, 2023).

The Emerging Market Context – Challenges and Opportunities

There is no single official definition or classification of what constitutes an emerging market economy. In general, we follow the broad definition proposed by Green Templeton College (n.d.) that emerging market economies are those that have made significant strides toward political, social, and economic progress in recent years but still face systemic issues with political instability and less developed and reliable systems and institutions. Examples of emerging market economies include India, China, Mexico, Russia, Turkey, Brazil, and other nations in regions such as the Middle East, Africa, and Southeast Asia.

In public sector digital transformation analyses in emerging economies, discussions of the barriers faced often focus on financial, infrastructure, and other resource barriers (Mustaf et al., 2020). Governments in emerging economies may lack the financial resources necessary to fund digitalization projects. Hence, public–private partnerships, third-sector funding, and global projects such as those run by the World Bank are crucial in ensuring these digital projects can progress (World Economic Forum & FTI Consulting, 2023). Even if financial resources are available, infrastructure remains a persistent concern in many emerging economies. Many emerging economies, such as those in Africa, struggle with maintaining a strong and consistent electricity supply, especially to rural areas, which negatively impacts internet connectivity (EWGDTEM, 2022).

Nevertheless, beyond these significant constraints, sociocultural and political factors play an equally decisive role in helping or hindering the success of public sector digital transformation (Dakduk et al., 2023). The uptake of technologies in any society is influenced and constrained by social factors affecting its users, such as economic status, education and literacy, cultural attitudes and beliefs, gender, age and generation, social norms, language and communication styles, and previous experiences with technologies (Gupta, 2023). Political factors play an equally crucial role, with government ideologies, laws, regulations, and international and domestic security and relations interacting with sociocultural factors to create a significant approach to how new technologies are developed, deployed, and used (OECD, 2021).

Sociocultural Challenges

Digital transformation in the public sector often involves creating digital programs and platforms that meet citizens' needs; doing so, however, first involves ensuring citizens can access the programs and platforms in the first place. One of the first significant accessibility concerns to consider is language. Even in today's increasingly globalized world, all nations still have a variety of ethnic groups and languages spoken. Emerging economies, perhaps more than others, have a high level of intra-national ethnic groups such as indigenous groups, tribal groups, and nomadic groups, which results in a high level of niche and locally spoken language (Maswanganyi, 2023). Many of these groups tend to be located in rural or remote areas with access issues, more so than in developed nations with high urbanization rates and more stable transport infrastructure (Matthess & Kunkel, 2020). India, for example, has over 2,000 ethnic groups and 122 major spoken languages (Encyclopedia Britannica, n.d.).

Platforms and programs need to be offered with multiple language interface options. Offering these media with only the official national language or a lingua franca, with possibly a narrow array of alternatives, marginalizes ethnic minority groups and indigenous groups, who may tend to live in rural areas and thus already face issues accessing government services (Elam, 2023). Many emerging economies have made efforts to make e-government platforms available in multiple languages, including regional and indigenous ones. In India, the Unified Mobile Application for New-age Governance (UMANG) supports twenty-three languages spoken by its population (National E-Government Division, n.d.).

Even when platforms and programs are made accessible, cultural resistance to such trends may still exist. In developed nations, digital technologies have been woven into the fabric of society for decades, with higher incomes and more developed national digital strategies leading to a deeper integration of technology in everyday life (Pomaza-Ponomarenko et al., 2020). In emerging economies, however, political and social instability and economic marginalization have led many to lag in the digital revolution and digital literacy (Pomaza-Ponomarenko et al., 2020). Thus, the digitalization of the public sector may be seen as new, threatening, or unusual, reflecting tensions between tradition and modernity and a lack of experience with technological literacy (Dakduk et al., 2023).

Cultural resistance is especially present when digital initiatives are introduced to rural citizens or those who follow a more traditional or tribal lifestyle. Groups that value community bonds, interpersonal relationships, and physical presence may resist using technology to access public services (Yavwa & Twinomurinzi, 2021). Technology may also be seen as a threat to traditional values and ways of life. Collectivistic cultures, common in emerging economies, reinforce this resistance; if technology is seen negatively or as a threat by group leaders, it can become stigmatized by other group members. The reverse can be leveraged – if technologies can be promoted as a status symbol, their adoption within the group can be accelerated (Dakduk et al., 2023). Addressing these barriers requires careful research, a thorough understanding of the group at hand, and appropriate tailoring of the technology's deployment. Digital initiatives must be flexible enough to suit the needs and characteristics of the cultural group (Gupta, 2023).

A lack of digital literacy and experience with technology can reinforce this resistance. A new way of accessing public services that is unfamiliar or complicated can be challenging to implement among certain groups, especially among members of older generations (da Silva et al., 2023). This phenomenon highlights the importance of introducing digital literacy education initiatives at various levels of society, from the school education system to local governance and community outreach (Allmann & Radu, 2023). Mexico is a prime example of the latter. In order to bridge the digital divide, in the early 2000s, the nation established Digital Community Centers in rural and remote areas that provide assisted access to the internet and information on the government and other institutions (OECD, 2008). The nation launched a similar project in 2010 to open digital learning centers in disadvantaged and isolated communities that offer courses in digital literacy and other areas of basic education (Apolitical, 2017). By 2014, over 130,000 individuals had graduated from courses offered by the centers (Apolitical, 2017).

In considering issues of accessibility, cultural resistance, and digital literacy, it is crucial to consider gender (Samuel et al., 2020). It is important to note that even in developed nations, women and girls tend to have less self-confidence in their digital technology skills and have a more negative perception of technology and its risks (European Institute for Gender Equality, 2020). However, in emerging economies, women and girls face significant physical and cultural barriers to accessing and using technology for public services. Women are more likely to have lower education, basic literacy, and digital literacy levels, hindering their ability to read and understand the information necessary for public services and use the technology they are offered (Malik, 2022).

Furthermore, traditional cultural norms tend to relegate women to the realm of the home and family care, whereas men are seen as responsible for earning a living. Thus, technology may be seen as less relevant to women's lives and needs (Mirkovski et al., 2023). Women's subservient social role in traditional cultures and less access to economic resources negatively impact whether they own a mobile phone or other digital devices (Rutashobya et al., 2021). In some traditional cultures, women's movements outside the home are also greatly restricted, limiting their opportunities to visit community centers or other public spaces outside the home where they may access digital public services (Malik, 2022).

Political Challenges

Aside from the complex sociocultural challenges that act as barriers to implementing public sector digital transformation projects, emerging economies also face numerous political hurdles. Developed nations often benefit from relatively stable political regimes, although it is essential to note that many developed nations have faced political instability and polarization in the last ten years (McCoy & Somer, 2021). Despite ideological conflicts, developed nations often have relatively stable democratic structures, having transitioned to mostly liberal democratic regimes in the previous century (Ketcham, 2021).

Emerging economies, however – many formerly under colonial rule – have faced these challenging transitions in either their recent history, now, or not yet for nations still under authoritarian rule (Karpenko et al., 2023). These transitions can lead to many governance challenges, such as corruption. In many emerging economies, funds that are meant to go toward digitalization initiatives are at risk of being stolen or misappropriated (Sadik-Zada et al., 2022). Funds may also be covertly redirected to other projects that fulfill governments' interests to a higher degree. Even if funds are directed and used accordingly, outdated and cumbersome bureaucracy can cause incremental delays and unnecessary red tape in getting projects off the ground (Sadik-Zada et al., 2022). Furthermore, corrupt and bureaucratic structures can lead to a lack of coordination between government departments and public sector entities, posing significant challenges as processes may be delayed, duplicated, or forgotten from one entity to the next (Kauma et al., 2022).

Political instability exacerbates a corrupt and bureaucratic governance system. Frequent changes in government, short political cycles, and civil unrest are common challenges in emerging economies, which can disrupt ongoing projects or deter international investment and cooperation regarding the projects in question (OECD, 2021). Political instability and civil unrest can also contribute to other challenges that stand in the way of digitalization, such as negatively impacting financial markets, increasing inflation, and damaging infrastructure such as a reliable electricity supply (Wandaogo, 2022). Shortened political cycles can encourage political leaders to direct their efforts toward short-term gains rather than long-term projects. Digitalization projects, especially in the realm of e-government, are particularly vulnerable in this regard because they are complex, long-term, and require the integration and coordination of multiple government departments (Malodia et al., 2021)

Additionally, several emerging economies are still under the rule of authoritarian governments, where control of enterprises, the economy, and infrastructure are centralized (Koop & Kessler, 2021). This form of governance poses unique challenges to implementing digitalization projects and ensuring citizens use the final digital outputs (OECD, 2021). The fact that digitalization projects enable greater public transparency and accountability is a point of contention for authoritarian states, which want to maintain opaque governance procedures (OECD, 2021).

Authoritarian governments also function on systems of censorship and surveillance. Digital platforms can become another tool for these governments to silence dissent or opposing views and collect data on citizens to surveil their movements and public expression (Huang & Tsai, 2022). Thus, digital initiatives may be either shut down, slowed down, or deliberately designed to further censorship and surveillance efforts. It is important to note that surveillance, censorship, and privacy issues are salient in developed and emerging nations (Padden, 2023). Developed nations have also been embroiled in scandals involving government surveillance of civilians; incidents have made cybersecurity and ethical use of data a growing concern and priority for nations around the globe (OECD, 2021).

Global international relations also play a significant role in the public digitalization projects of emerging economies. Governments in developed nations may be able to fund public digitalization initiatives on their own through taxpayer funds or other sources, with occasional support from international organizations or projects (Di Giulio & Vecchi, 2023). Emerging economies, nevertheless, are even more reliant on private partners, NGOs, international organizations, and the like to fund and provide infrastructure for public digitalization initiatives (EWGDTEM, 2022). Nevertheless, international funding and partnerships may be inaccessible to emerging economies struggling with the governance issues already mentioned, especially those still under the rule of authoritarian governments (OECD, 2021).

Overcoming Sociocultural and Political Roadblocks: Best Practices for Increasing the Success of Digitalization Initiatives

Although these challenges can pose significant barriers to implementing digitalization in the public sector in emerging economies, they are not insurmountable. Numerous best practices can be integrated into a multifaceted, inclusive, and ethically sound digitalization approach. Firstly, overcoming sociocultural challenges relating to access, inclusion, and cultural resistance involves careful research and community engagement during the development phase (OECD, 2023). We propose the following steps for implementing community engagement during a digitalization initiative:

1 Preliminary Research and Planning

Understand the Context
The organization behind the project should conduct a situational analysis to gain a greater understanding of the community and its political, cultural, and socioeconomic conditions (Onsongo, 2023). Existing literacy levels and digital infrastructure should be cataloged, as well as past digitalization efforts, their success levels, and how they were received in the community.

Stakeholder Identification
Critical stakeholders in the local community should be identified and mapped according to their interests, influence, and impact regarding the project. These stakeholders may include NGOs, local organizations, respected elders or other figures in the community, local governance officials, and citizens themselves (Dakduk et al., 2023).

Defining Objectives

The project's objectives should be clearly defined and made measurable in relation to the community at hand, including details on how the success of these objectives will be evaluated (surveys, interviews, metrics, etc.).

2 Building Partnerships and Trust

Engaging Local Leaders and Influencers

Local leaders and influencers in the community, who may or may not overlap with the critical stakeholders, should be approached for collaboration opportunities. These figures can use their networks and knowledge to build trust between the community members and the organization behind the project (Dakduk et al., 2023).

Transparent Communication

Honest and open communication channels and messages should be established early on. Community members need to be informed about the project processes, goals, and outcomes and be given opportunities to ask questions and have their concerns addressed (Gupta, 2023). This process can be facilitated through meetings in local community centers or through word-of-mouth among community members and local leaders.

3 Inclusive Engagement Strategies

Inclusivity and Accessibility

Communications about the project, as well as the aspects of the project itself, must be inclusive of all community members. Media channels can be used (such as local radio and social media). However, the project must also consider the digital divide as well as how to reach diverse groups often ignored in such projects, such as women, the elderly, the disabled, nomadic groups, lower social castes, and ethnic minorities (Onsongo, 2023). Earlier research on the community will help inform various tactics at this stage.

Participatory Approaches

Organizing community workshops, focus groups, and town hall meetings can all be used to pilot different stages of the project and gather input and feedback in an agile approach, where user feedback is collected at every stage of the development and deployment process, refining the final product/output in a cyclical, holistic process (Ciancarini et al., 2024). Some favored participatory approaches include scenario planning, role-playing, and brainstorming sessions.

Digital Tools and Digital Literacy Training

As the project is being developed, digital tools can be used to engage community members and gradually acclimate them to using digital technologies on an everyday basis (OECD, 2023). In-person meetings and focus groups can introduce tools and platforms, such as mobile devices, that facilitate interactive polls, surveys, and online forums. Training sessions and programs can also be offered to improve community members' digital literacy. Private–public partnerships are valuable in providing the resources, settings, and trainers needed to facilitate such programs

4 Post-Implementation

Developing Evaluation Metrics
Key performance indicators (KPIs) should be implemented to track the success of community engagement activities and the overall project itself. Both quantitative and qualitative methods should be used to assess success.

Feedback
Follow up on feedback provided by community members and keep feedback channels open during and after the project's implementation. This continuous stream of feedback allows the organization to understand whether the project is meeting community members' needs and whether certain aspects need to be adjusted, removed, or radically changed (OECD, 2023).

Sustaining Community Engagement
Keep the communication channels, training initiatives, and other community engagement activities active even after the project has been implemented and evaluated. These activities provide value to local communities and will ease the process of introducing future digitalization initiatives later on (Allmann & Radu, 2023).

Overcoming the barriers posed by an unstable or authoritarian political environment can be more challenging, but there are tactics to make digitalization projects more attractive to such governments. The initial framework discussed in this section can be applied but with careful revisions along the following points:

1 Preliminary Research and Planning

Political and Economic Context
Preliminary research must involve a thorough analysis of the economic and political context at hand, including the history of the country or region, fundamental governance structures, recent changes in political leadership, and current influential actors (OECD, 2021).

Risk Assessment
A thorough risk assessment must be conducted regarding governance and political stability, including issues of government surveillance, censorship, and international relations (Huang & Tsai, 2022). This assessment should include contingency plans and risk mitigation strategies, especially in scenarios of government collapse, snap elections, infrastructure failure, or war and conflict.

Defining Objectives
The project's objectives should align with modernization or development agendas that have government support. This stage requires a careful balance of government interests with broader democratic or developmental goals.

2 Building Partnerships and Trust

Engaging Stakeholders
Stakeholders in government and other political structures should be identified and mapped, with careful consideration of their political interests and alliances. Identifying and partnering with international organizations can be valuable in this regard, as they can provide stability and guidance to ground a project in the longer term (World Economic Forum & FTI Consulting, 2023).

Tailored Communication
Although communication about the project should be transparent, it should also be tailored to the political environment at hand. Initial proposals for such projects can be tailored to emphasize quick wins, short-term implementation, and visible benefits to align with short-term political cycles (Schlogl & Kim, 2023). Numerous short-term projects can build momentum toward a larger goal or program, with each small project accomplishing one part of the goal or building and refining the foundations for a larger project.

Areas of Focus
Proposing digitalization projects to or within authoritarian governments should begin by focusing on areas or sectors that are non-threatening to governance structures, such as education, healthcare, and agriculture (Karpenko et al., 2023). Proposals should emphasize the business case and economic benefits of digitalization, aspects that are agreeable to governments from various parts of the political spectrum.

Coordination
Once projects are in development, the project management process needs to encourage interdepartmental collaboration and consistency. Digital

transformation initiatives should be governed by a central coordination body, such as a dedicated task force, committee, or agency (Wouters et al., 2023). The body should also set project goals and standards; it might be helpful to follow successful public digitalization cases from other nations or best practices from international organizations. The body should establish an overarching digital strategy developed through a collaborative process involving all stakeholders.

3 Post-Implementation

Developing Evaluation Metrics
Key performance indicators (KPIs) can be used to track the success of the project using quantitative and qualitative methods in evaluation. The criteria defining the success of the project should be adjusted according to the unique political situation of the nation or region at hand. Results should be reported in a low-profile manner and confined to government officials and any other stakeholders who have provided funding for the project (Schlogl & Kim, 2023).

Long-Term Sustainability
The long-term sustainability of digitalization projects can be a challenging prospect in unstable or authoritarian political environments. Funding should be secured from diverse sources, including international bodies or organizations, to reduce dependency on a single government or body that may lose power. The project should also remain politically neutral to ensure its survival in the face of changing political leadership. Cybersecurity safeguards are also crucial, given the instability of many emerging economies' digital infrastructure (Hammerschmid et al., 2023).

Conclusions

Emerging economies may struggle to compete with developed nations regarding infrastructure and stable governance and often struggle with unique sociocultural challenges, but these barriers do not have to permanently bar them from accessing the benefits of digitalization. The public sector is one of the most crucial areas in which to begin digitalization efforts in emerging economies. Digitalizing public functions and services creates a more transparent, efficient, and innovative governance structure to help emerging economies increase their participation and competitiveness in the global economic, social, and political landscape. Adequate funding and international support are not enough to ensure digitalization efforts are carried out to fruition. In order to surmount sociocultural and political barriers, digitalization initiatives need to be conducted with a mindset of understanding the culture of a nation's citizens and its public sector and striking a balance between addressing unique cultural needs and introducing new ideas and procedures to institute gradual culture change. It is an effort that requires a holistic and agile mindset and an innovative vision that can project the future of these nations and the role that digitalization can play in making those futures brighter.

3 Emerging Market Contexts

Context matters in understanding organizational development and policy formulation. Specifically, the socioeconomic environment in which digitalization takes place has a profound impact on policy practices. In order to offer meaningful insights for digitalization strategy, analysis must consider the economic context, including factors such as economic stability, market conditions, and institutional robustness. In this vein, this section outlines the emerging market context in which digitalization takes place. Digitalization in emerging markets is a recent phenomenon that takes place in a fundamentally different institutional context to that of developed economies. In turn, this presents a process of digitalization as well as a set of outcomes from digitalization which is both idiosyncratic and different from those in developed countries. While it is probable that public sector digitalization in emerging markets offers potential for a step change in the efficiency, reach and impact of the public sector, institutional weaknesses and uneven socioeconomic development typical of emerging markets, create risks and the potential for failure of such initiatives.

In light of what has been discussed, this section is organized as follows. First is a section which describes and evaluates the notion of emerging markets in a historical and contemporary context. It illustrates the most salient characteristics of what emerging markets are. Second, we explore one of the key features of emerging markets: institutional voids. Institutional maturity (or lack thereof) play a key role in the framing and execution of digitalization initiatives which we address in the third section where we offer insights into how this impacts digitalization in the emerging markets. Fourth, in the context of the notion of technology leapfrogging, we provide a brief overview of digitalization policy initiatives for emerging markets which provide a basis for a considerably more in-depth country-comparative discussion in sections four and five of our Element.

What Are Emerging Markets?

Analogously with the pervasive influence of globalization, the idea of emerging markets has evolved into one of the most widespread and indispensable concepts in our contemporary era. An extensive body of research has delved into the notion, structure, and modalities of emerging markets. According to Rottig & Torres de Oliveira (2019), the original story of the term "emerging markets" was coined in 1981 by Antoine van Agtmael during a meeting at the Salomon Brothers Investment Bank, proposing a new global investment fund. Definitions of emerging markets abound in the literature. For instance, Rottig (2016) defines them as markets with less institutional development in contrast to developed economies. Hoskisson et al. (2013) characterize emerging markets by high GDP growth and robust government support for liberalization policies. Khanna and Palepu (2010) depict emerging markets as transitional economies moving from relatively closed to relatively open economic systems as well as emphasizing salient characteristics such as low and middle incomes of the typical consumer in emerging markets; weak market capitalization and capital accumulation relative to developed economies and a lack of liquidity in financial asset markets.

Continuous higher-than-world average economic growth is a hallmark of emerging markets, with studies indicating growth rates consistently surpassing the global average (Hoskisson, 2000; Khanna et al., 2005; Khanna, 2009; Radjou & Prabhu, 2012; Satoglu, 2020). Global comparisons also reveal that GDP growth rates in emerging markets outpace those in developed economies (IMF, 2021). The expectation is that emerging markets should continue to drive global growth in the years ahead, continuing to provide increasingly reliable sources of skilled labor and new, disruptive technologies (Horwitz et al., 2015). This growth trajectory presents opportunities for increasing investments in the digitalization of public institutions and national policy infrastructures. Historically, emerging markets have also served as crucial sources for raw materials, low-cost labor, and in more recent decades, emerging markets have become attractive product and service markets for developed economy firms. Since the turn of the twenty-first century, emerging market sustained growth has further transformed them into hubs for complex manufacturing and services, offering ongoing opportunities for MNCs (Cavusgil et al., 2018). Nine investment indices, including IMF, BRICS+ Next Eleven, FTSE, MSCI, SandP, EM bond index, Dow Jones, Russell, and Columbia University EMGP, have been developed to showcase emerging market investment opportunities based on diverse criteria sustainability of growth, quality of infrastructure and ease of inward/outward capital flow to name a few. The following section provides more details on what are believed to be the key characteristics of emerging markets.

Emerging markets are economies in the process of rapid growth and industrialization, typically characterized by transitioning from low-income to middle-income status. These markets are called "emerging" because they are still developing and haven't yet reached the level of economic development and stability comparable with developed economies. Emerging markets can be found across various regions of the world, and research has identified certain common features. First, emerging markets often experience faster economic growth rates compared to developed countries and are undergoing a process of catch-up with developed economies. Economic growth experienced in emerging markets is typically associated with factors such as increased industrialization and the arrival of a consumerist middle class. Second, is the phenomenon of rapid urbanization. As people move from rural areas to cities in search of better opportunities, better social and health infrastructure, emerging markets exhibit significant urbanization. According to UN data, India, China, and Nigeria will collectively contribute to thirty-five percent of the anticipated increase in the global urban population from 2018 to 2050. Projections indicate that India is expected to witness an addition of 416 million urban residents, China 255 million, and Nigeria 189 million during this period (Henderson & Turner, 2020). This shift leads to increased demand for adequate housing, transport infrastructure, and consumer goods and services. It also creates a huge burden for governments who are expected to meet this urban growth with adequate social infrastructure and public services.

Third, many emerging markets are rich in natural resources, including oil, minerals, and agricultural products contributing fundamental inputs to downstream complex manufacturing and services. At early stages of an emerging market's development, these natural resources can be a significant driver of economic growth and exports but over time are expected to be eclipsed by the emergence of manufacturing and service industries. Fourth, demographic trends in emerging markets are especially salient as emerging markets often have a younger and faster growing population compared to developed countries. This demographic factor contributes to an abundant workforce, growing consumption potential and innovation and entrepreneurship. Fifth, as the "growing pains" of emerging markets continue, pressure of governments to make significant investment in infrastructure including transportation, energy, and telecommunications rises. This creates opportunities for domestic and foreign companies to participate in the numerous public procurement and tendering processes required to build the infrastructure.

Some of the most well-known emerging markets include countries like China, India, Brazil, Russia (often referred to as the BRIC nations), as well as many countries in Southeast Asia (Indonesia, Vietnam, Thailand), Africa (Egypt, Ethiopia and Nigeria), and Latin America (Colombia, Argentina and

Uruguay). While these markets have in common shown substantial economic growth and development in recent years, there remains considerable heterogeneity across emerging markets. Sources of heterogeneity include demographic growth, geo-political context, and uneven levels of democratization which implies that each of these countries will face idiosyncratic economic and social challenges as they continue to develop.

Institutional theory plays a pivotal role in understanding emerging markets. Institutional theory research, dating back to 1980, focuses on how an organization's institutional environment influences business performance. Friedland and Alford (1991) define "institutional logic" as a set of beliefs, practices, values, assumptions, and rules determining what is meaningful and legitimate in a given field. Seen by firms as "background conditions," Arnold and Quelch (1998) and taken largely for granted in developed economies, institutional development, efficiency and maturity define the competitive landscape for firms and shape strategic responses to the institutional context. Put another way, firms can rely upon supporting institutions in developed economies to facilitate their business strategies and operations. By contrast, institutional gaps, weaknesses and inefficiencies in emerging markets require firms operating in these countries to find ways to fill or "correct" institutional weaknesses by building or internalizing external institutional processes. This reality requires scholarship on emerging markets to focus on theories adjacent to institutional theory such as agency theory, transaction-cost theory, resource-based theory and so on. Again, in the context of digitalization, emerging market governments can leapfrog traditional institutional development and its associated bureaucratic frictions by embracing various features of "e-government" which enhances relationship between citizens and residents of the country with the government. It also positively impacts numerous aspects of "doing business" by speeding up, streamlining and simplifying a plethora of processes associated with establishing businesses in the country. The next section of our section explicitly addresses the *sine qua non* of emerging markets: institutional voids.

Institutional Voids

Khanna and Palepu (1997) first introduced the concept of institutional voids to describe the structural weaknesses that set emerging markets apart from their more developed counterparts. This concept supports the idea that firms entering emerging markets need to adjust their strategies and reconfigure their existing resources and capabilities. Arnold and Quelch (1998) emphasized that emerging markets are characterized by unfamiliar conditions and problems including inadequately functioning or non-existent logistical infrastructure (such as high-ways, railways, harbors, airports, and ICT networks), weak market systems and distribution channels, and significant variations in consumer behavior that can be challenging for companies from developed countries to comprehend and adapt to. Institutional voids are believed to create both entry barriers and limitations on a firm's commitment in emerging markets. A weak institutional environment, characterized by high institutional voids, can discourage firms from dedicating time and resources to these markets, as observed in studies by Broadman et al. (2004) and Welter and Smallbone (2011).

Institutions are commonly segmented into formal (e.g., policies, rules) and informal (e.g., culture, norms) types, that exert varying impacts on business and investment activity. Firms depend on market intermediaries in developed economies such as payment processors, asset valuers, and legal and arbitration service providers but operating in emerging markets poses challenges due to lower-quality institutions. Institutional voids can be further categorized into market exchange, political and social systems, and openness, presenting both challenges and also business opportunities for firms. Recognizing a market's relative level of institutional development enables firms to better navigate the impact of weak institutional environments.

Institutional voids, in the context of emerging markets, refer to the absence of or inadequacy of key institutions and regulatory frameworks that are typically found in developed or mature economies. These voids can pose significant challenges and risks for businesses and investors operating in emerging markets. Institutional voids can manifest in various ways. First, legal and regulatory frameworks in emerging markets may suffer from poor definitions and consistency both in formulation and enforcement. This can create uncertainty and make it difficult for businesses to navigate legal issues, such as contract enforcement and intellectual property protection. Second, it relates to the recognition and protection of private property rights. Weak property rights and inadequate protection of intellectual property can deter foreign investment and harm incentives for new product development, innovation and new technology. Third relates to financial and capital markets infrastructure. Emerging markets often lack a developed financial infrastructure which typically comprises efficient, transparent banking and payments systems, diverse and affordable credit markets, as well as well-functioning, liquid stock exchanges and related financial asset marketplaces. This can make it challenging for businesses to access capital, raising the cost of capital in the emerging markets relative to developed countries. Financial market and institutional voids also complicate financial risk management as the ability to hedge financial risk relies upon the availability and consistency of financial data. Fourth, weak or non-existent contract enforcement is another important institutional void: inconsistent or unreliable contract enforcement mechanisms can make it difficult for businesses to engage in long-term agreements or investments and make business dispute resolution highly unpredictable and costly.

Fifth, the pervasive incidence of corruption in emerging markets can increase the cost of doing business, creating an uneven playing field faced by firms, and deters foreign investment. At a minimum, it raises the informal cost of doing business and exposes firms to legal risk by requiring their executives to engage with public officials in an opaque manner. Sixth, logistics infrastructure and associated operational transparency. Insufficient logistical and energy infrastructure raises operational costs and limits the distribution and market reach of businesses. This is especially acute in the so-called "last mile" context where firms face highly fragmented and uneven distribution systems. Plummer (2015) reports UN data suggesting that as many as four billion people in the world do not have addresses – the vast majority of whom are in developing countries and emerging markets.

Khanna, Palepu, and Sinha (2005) developed a formal taxonomy of potential institutional voids, dividing them into five groups. First are political and social systems: This group considers the overall political stability of a country, the protection of private property and intellectual rights, and the effectiveness of the judicial system. Second are institutional voids that limit market transparency and openness. This group focuses primarily on the existence of discriminatory legal restrictions and constraints facing foreign investors relative to local ones. The third set of voids relate to product markets. This involves thinness of data on consumers and the ease of access to valuable information on consumers and market trends, the existence of an adequate distribution system, and the extent of product-related environmental and safety regulations. Fourth, there are a plethora of institutional voids related to labor markets. This category concerns the consistency and quality of labor market regulation as well as the availability and quality of human capital. The latter is closely related to the quality of the education and professional formation system in the country. Lastly the fifth and final category of institutional voids identified relate to capital markets. This category considers the extent and quality of financial intermediaries, venture capital investors, stock markets, and financial reporting and regulatory systems.

Emerging Markets and Digitalization

The process by which less developed countries become emerging markets is intimately connected to the digitalization of their societies, governments and economy. Digitalization in emerging markets contributes to economic development by increasing transparency and efficiency, at its core lowering the cost of economic exchange in the country. In particular, public-sector initiatives in emerging markets that involve digitalization bring numerous advantages. Public sector digitalization can significantly enhance economic development through various mechanisms. E-government initiatives, such as online portals, digital identity systems, and electronic communication channels, streamline government-citizen interactions. This enhances the overall service delivery experience, reduces bureaucratic red tape, and encourages a more business-friendly environment.

First, digitalization streamlines public sector processes, eliminating or reducing bureaucratic hurdles leading to enhanced efficiency. Automated systems, digital records, and online services contribute to faster decision-making and more productive government operations. These efficiency gains lead to cost savings and resource optimization to both the public sector and private sector participants.

Second, digital platforms facilitate greater transparency in government operations in emerging markets. Accessible and real-time data on public spending, policies, and performance enhance public sector accountability to citizens, residents, and investors. This transparency in turn exposes corruption with a potential for greater deterrence of graft, bribery and other forms of corruption. This fosters citizen trust in government institutions and enhances an emerging market's reputation to foreign investors and international diplomatic partners. Third, digitalization promotes innovation in public service delivery and policy-making in emerging markets. Open data initiatives, digital platforms, and technology-driven solutions create an environment conducive to risk taking, more strategic decision-making and greater entrepreneurship. This, in turn, stimulates economic growth by fostering a culture of innovation and supporting the development of tech-driven industries in emerging markets. Fourth, public sector digitalization in emerging markets improves citizens' access to public services. Online platforms and mobile applications associated with e-government enable easy and quick access to government services, reducing the barriers for citizens and businesses to interact with the public sector. This accessibility can lead to increased participation in socioeconomic activities.

Fifth, as part of a program of public infrastructure development, public digitization plays a crucial role in planning and implementing infrastructure projects in emerging markets. Advanced data analytics, smart city initiatives, and digital mapping contribute to more effective infrastructure development. Improved infrastructure, in turn, supports economic activities by providing a robust foundation for businesses to thrive. Sixth, data-driven public sector decision making is a key feature of public digitalization in emerging markets. Digitalization generates vast amounts of data that can be utilized for informed decision-making by the public sector. Data analytics and business intelligence tools enable civil servants and policymakers to analyze trends, identify areas for improvement, and implement targeted policies that promote economic development. Lastly, emerging markets that embrace public sector digitalization often achieve greater competitiveness on the global stage. A digitally advanced public sector attracts foreign investment, fosters international collaboration, and positions the country as a leader in the global digital economy. In summary, public-sector digitalization in emerging markets contributes to economic development by enhancing efficiency, promoting innovation, improving transparency, and fostering an environment conducive to investment and entrepreneurship. The integration of digital technologies into emergent market government operations has the potential to create a more agile, responsive, and economically vibrant society.

Despite the many benefits to emerging markets from the embracing of public sector digitalization, there are also challenges associated with it which policymakers should be clearly mindful of. First, in some regions and contexts in emerging markets, reliable access to digital infrastructure is hampered by patchy distribution of internet and related ICT assets. World Bank data reports that around one third of sub-Saharan Africa populations has access to the Internet which pales in comparison with North America where the vast majority of citizens and residents benefit from reliable internet access (Fomba Kamga et al., 2022). This slows the adoption of digital technologies and the reach and efficiency of e-government. Second, while emerging market governments may wish to embrace public sector digitalization, there are vast disparities in digital literacy in emerging markets, creating a digital divide, with only segments of the population in emerging markets benefiting from digitalization initiatives (Ameen and Gorman, 2009). Malamud et al. (2019) reported that internet access is ubiquitous for children in developed countries with more than 95 percent of fifteen-year-old students in OECD countries having a reliable link to the internet at home. By contrast, fewer than half of fifteen-year-old students in a selection of developing countries (Algeria, Peru, and Vietnam) had access to the internet at home. While this access in emerging markets is increasing quite rapidly, the need for enhanced digital literacy remains significant. Third, as digital adoption grows, so do the risks of cyberattacks and privacy breaches, which can have significant consequences including financial loss, the spread of disinformation and "fake news." Fourth, related to this is an absence of reliable and predictable data protection frameworks and regulations which undermines trust in government among populaces in emerging markets.

The overarching theme for the development of public sector digitalization in emerging markets is to embrace technology leapfrogging which is central to overcoming these institutional voids. Technology leapfrogging involves the integration and deployment of new and advanced technologies with the aim of bypassing historically intermediate steps in technological development. This concept is especially relevant for emerging markets that can seize the opportunity to embrace the latest developments in digitalization without following the same, gradual pathway that more developed nations experienced in the past. Leapfrogging also allows for a swift and accelerated adoption of digital technologies, allowing emerging markets to pursue catch up or even surpassing more technologically advanced counterparts in developed countries.

While in Sections 4 and 5, we will discuss in much more detail digitalization across a range of emerging market countries, both at a strategic level as well as policy specific areas and initiatives in public sector, we summarize the types of initiatives. First are the development of centralized online platforms for citizens to access government services, information, and resources known as e-government portals. These are aimed at creating seamless, integrated access to a range of government services for citizens, residents and investors. These would include online portals for tax filing, business registration, and permit applications, radically simplifying bureaucratic processes. Second, are the creation and deployment of digital identity system designed to enhance authentication and secure access to government services. Among the benefits of digital IDs are the ability to better target and streamline social welfare distribution and reduce identity fraud. Notwithstanding, digital IDs in emerging markets should be accompanied by strong data and privacy protections. Third, given the explosive growth in emerging markets in the use of mobile devices such as smart phones, access to e-government services for billions of people is through their mobile devices. Sometimes termed "m-government," it comprises the development and roll-out of mobile applications for citizens to access government services and receive timely information through SMS-based services for communication, alerts, and reminders, which is particularly relevant and useful in rural areas.

Fourth, as access to traditional education institutions in emerging markets may be limited due to the need for significant fixed asset and real estate development, public e-education initiatives involves the integration of digital technologies in education systems, including e-learning platforms and digital classrooms. Online educational resources to improve access to quality education in remote areas is especially relevant. Experiences with COVID-19 digital learning has provided roadmaps for the development and rollout of public e-education. Fifth, the digitization of healthcare and social welfare services is also an important component of public sector digitalization. Among a range of related aspects, the development of digital health and social welfare records and AI-centered, data driven systems to improve the quality of healthcare and social services and delivery. Furthermore, mobile applications for appointment scheduling, telemedicine consultations, and health information dissemination are obvious applications for e-healthcare. Electronic transfer of social welfare payments to citizens could reduce leakages and allow for timely and accurate transfers of financial support. Sixth, given the fact that in some emerging markets, substantial portions of the population are involved in agriculture, smart agriculture technologies such as digital platforms providing farmers with information on weather, market prices, and sharing of agricultural knowledge and best practices could be a valuable public digitalization initiative. Additionally, mobile apps for farmers to access financial services, marketplaces, and agricultural extension services could also enhance productivity of the farming sector in emerging markets.

Seventh, while digital financial inclusion in emerging markets is a core goal of private banking and finance institutions, government initiatives in this space can play a supporting roll through the development of digital finance infrastructure through the central bank system of the country. Eighth, with the rapid growth of urban populations in emerging markets, the need for better city planning becomes imperative. Implementation of smart city initiatives to enhance urban infrastructure and services. Digital mapping and planning tools to improve urban development and resource management. Lastly, as governments are commonly the single biggest buyer of goods and services, the creation of e-procurement systems to enhance transparency and efficiency in government procurement processes could reduce corruption in public tendering and make more effective use of public funds in emerging markets. Online bidding platforms for vendors to participate in government procurement can also facilitate the development of digital databases to specify tenders more accurately.

All in all, these applications of digitalization in the public sector contribute to more efficient governance, improved service delivery, and enhanced opportunities for socioeconomic development in developing countries.

Conclusion

This section has considered public sector digitalization in the context of emerging markets. While the lack of prosperity and numerous forms of inequality in emerging markets relative to developed countries presents evident challenges in the development of e-government initiatives, we argue that a key prospect for emerging market governments is to embrace digital technology leapfrogging opportunities that will allow them to bypass traditional public sector scaling-up and capacity building and overcome institutional voids which are ever present in emerging markets. There is an extensive agenda of initiatives available to emerging market governments ranging from mobile applications to offer government services, to integrated, transparent e-tendering. In the following two sections, we will examine comparative models for e-government and their implications for best practice in e-government design for emerging markets.

4 Comparative Models for e-Government

This section will look at the "by design" principle for e-government initiatives, the key criteria necessary for successful e-government, the role of organizational and bureaucratic culture in the development of e-government and a comparison of some countries already using e-government and finally at some current and emerging trends in e-government.

By-Design Principles

The "by design" principles in e-government aim to improve the efficiency, transparency, and effectiveness of government services using digital technologies. They reflect a commitment to leveraging digital technology, incorporating specific characteristics and considerations in the design and implementation of digital government to deliver better services and promote trust between citizens and the government. These principles emphasize integrating key considerations into the design and development of e-government systems and processes from the outset, rather than as afterthoughts. These include digital by design, privacy by design, open by design and automated by design. They are essential for building and maintaining effective e-government systems that meet the evolving needs of citizens while upholding principles of privacy, transparency, efficiency, and accessibility. Furthermore, they should be user-centric and secure.

The **Digital by Design** principle emphasizes that digital technologies should be central to the design of government services and operations, that government services and operations are planned, developed, and executed with a "digital-first" approach in mind ensuring that digital channels and technologies are at the core of service delivery. This leads to more accessible and user-friendly services for citizens and businesses. It involves the strategic use of technology to enhance service delivery and accessibility. Some key aspects include the utilization of modern digital technologies, such as data analytics, mobile applications, and cloud computing to improve service delivery. To ensure equitable access to digital government services, it is essential to promote digital literacy skills among citizens, that government websites and online portals are accessible, user-friendly, and responsive.

Privacy by design is a framework that promotes the integration of privacy and data protection measures into the design and architecture of government systems and services. It emphasizes the need to consider privacy as a fundamental requirement and implements strong data protection measures such as encryption and user consent mechanisms. Some other aspects include minimizing the collection and retention of data to only what is strictly necessary for the intended purpose, providing transparency to citizens regarding data usage and privacy policy, and conducting Privacy Impact Assessments (PIAs) to identify and mitigate potential privacy risks.

Open by design encourages governments to adopt principles of transparency, openness, and accessibility of government data and processes. It promotes citizen engagement through open government initiatives, such as open policy-making and crowdsourcing. Open by design implies that government data and information is made readily available to the public in open and machine-readable formats, fostering transparency, innovation, and public participation. It entails publishing government data as open data, which is not only accessible to the public, but also to developers for reuse and innovation. These open standards and interoperable systems facilitate data sharing and collaboration between government agencies.

Automated by Design involves e-government systems incorporate the use of automation technologies, such as artificial intelligence (AI), to streamline government processes. These could include chatbots and virtual assistants to enhance citizen interactions and support services, leading to more efficient and streamlined processes for services such as permitting, licensing, and information retrieval. Automated by Design uses data analytics and predictive modelling to make data-driven decisions and allocation of resources more effective. Automated by Design requires careful consideration of ethical and accountability issues with regards to automated decision-making, especially in areas like welfare and law enforcement.

Key e-Government Criteria

As already mentioned, Electronic Government, or e-government, stands for the use of digital technology and the internet employed by the government for the delivery of services, processes and interaction with citizens, businesses, and other government entities. For its effective delivery several key criteria should be included. First, *accessibility* of e-government services are reachable to all citizens, with multiple channels for interaction, including those with disabilities and those in rural or remote areas with limited access to technology. Second, services and websites should be *user-friendly* and designed with user needs and preferences in mind. User-centric design principles help ensure that users can intuitively easily navigate and interact with government platforms. Third, e-government should have *robust cybersecurity measures* to protect the confidentiality, integrity, and availability of user data as well as complying with data privacy laws and regulations ensuring that user data is safe and public trust is maintained. Fourth, government agencies should aim for *interoperability*, ensuring that different government systems and databases can seamlessly work together and share data. This helps prevent duplication of efforts and improves efficiency. Fifth, e-government should have *secure and convenient payment options* to facilitate online payments and transactions for government services, fees, taxes, and fines. Sixth, e-government should *promote transparency in government operations* by giving the public access to government information, decision-making processes, and budgets. In addition, government information and datasets should be in open and machine-readable formats.

These general principles should be enhanced with specific actions as follows:

1. **Digital Identity and Authentication:** Implement secure and reliable methods of verifying the identities of businesses and users online. Enable users to access a range of e-government services with a single digital identity.
2. **Digital Inclusion:** Provide digital literacy training and ensure internet access is available everywhere to ensure that all members of the public have access to the necessary technology and skills to participate in e-government services.
3. **Cross-Agency Collaboration:** The reduction of bureaucratic silos is essential to enable collaboration, coordination and streamline processes among government agencies. This avoids duplication and provides a seamless experience for the public to complete multiple transactions or access information through a single portal.
4. **Legal and Regulatory Framework:** Establish a clear legal and regulatory framework, ensuring that e-government follows and complies with, existing laws and regulations, governs e-government initiatives, including laws related to data protection, cybersecurity, digital signatures and electronic transactions.
5. **Scalability and Future-Readiness:** E-government systems need to be designed to cater for growth, technological advancements and adaptable to changing user needs.
6. **Cross-Platform Accessibility:** E-government services should be optimized to allow accessibility across all devices and platforms, and to develop mobile apps when appropriate to accommodate the use of smartphones and tablets.

7. **Capacity Building and Education:** Provide training and capacity-building programs for government employees to effectively manage and deliver e-government services. Government agencies should promote digital literacy and engage in public awareness campaigns and educational initiatives to inform businesses and users about available e-government services and how to use them effectively.

8. **Collaboration and Partnerships:** Develop public–private partnerships and collaborate with civil society, and international organizations to leverage expertise and resources. Incorporate lessons-learned from other countries in new initiatives.

9. **Budget and Sustainability:** For the development and maintenance of e-government infrastructure it is necessary to allocate the necessary budget and resources to ensure long-term sustainability and scalability of e-government initiatives.

10. **Feedback, Measurement, and Evaluation:** Incorporates mechanisms for users to provide feedback, report issues, and collect data to access the effectiveness of e-government services. This helps to identify changing needs, continuously refine and improve services, and address concerns promptly. E-government services need to be regularly assessed and evaluated to measure their effectiveness and impact, leading to improvements and better service delivery.

These criteria can be considered as a foundation for the successful execution of e-government initiatives, helping governments in fostering greater inclusivity, efficiency, and effectiveness in citizen engagement while enhancing digital governance as they deliver essential services.

Countries Using e-Government Successfully

The following section provides a *tour d'horizon* of selected countries with emerging economies in each region that have systematically attempted to develop a comprehensive e-government strategy. These countries have largely been regarded as having succeeded in their attempts to develop e-government. Table 1 summarizes the key areas that e-government strategies should focus on and the degree to which the countries surveyed have accomplished or met those criteria.

Estonia

Having implemented a range of innovative digital solutions and policies to enhance government services, streamline administrative processes, and promote transparency, Estonia gained a reputation as one of the most digitally

Table 1 Comparison of e-government service offered

	Estonia	India	Rwanda	South Korea	UAE	Uruguay
Citizen Digital ID	✓			✓	✓	✓
Digital Authentication / Signature	✓	✓		✓		✓
Centralized Public Services Portal	✓		✓	✓	✓	✓
Interoperability / Integrated Data Centers	✓		✓	✓		✓
Legal and Regulatory Framework	✓		✓		✓	✓
Robust Data Security and Privacy Protection	✓				✓	✓
User-centric Design	✓			✓	✓	
Open Data (in machine readable format)	✓	✓			✓	✓
MyGov (citizen engagement with Government)	✓				✓	✓
Digital Voting	✓	✓				
Passport Service	✓	✓				
Residency Permit	✓			✓		
Visitor e-Visa Services	No	✓				
Cross-platform Accessibility	✓	✓	✓	✓	✓	
Digital Payments (e.g., Tax / Fees / Fines)	✓	✓	✓	✓	✓	✓
Digital Access to Health Services	✓	✓		✓	✓	✓
Digital Access to Education	✓	✓		✓		✓
Digital Police	✓					

Table 1 (cont.)

Digital Justice (access to courts)	√					√
Digital Land Registry	√	√				
Smart City	√		√			
Online Business Registration	√		√			
Digital Inclusion / Literacy Programs	√		√		√	√
Partnerships	√	√	√	√		√
Government e-Marketplace / e-Procurement	√	√	√	√		√
Measurement and Evaluation	√¹					
Scalability and Future-Readiness	√					
Feedback Mechanism for Improvement	√					

Source: Authors' Own.
¹Not central, each institution conducts their own surveys.

advanced countries in the world. Its success in e-government can be attributed to its commitment to digital innovation, a strong legal framework for digital identity and data protection, and a culture of trust in government services.

India

The first national e-Governance Plan (NeGP) was launched in 2006 to improve public service delivery using ICT. In 2015, the Digital India Initiative aimed at transforming India into a digitally empowered society and knowledge economy. It focuses on providing digital infrastructure, delivering services electronically, and promoting digital literacy. India has made significant strides in implementing e-government initiatives to enhance the delivery of public services, promote transparency, and increase efficiency. The country's approach to e-government involves collaboration between central and state governments, as well as partnerships with the private sector. While significant progress has been made, challenges such as digital literacy, internet access in remote areas, and data privacy concerns remain to be tackled as India continues to expand and improve its e-government initiatives.

Rwanda

The Rwandan government's commitment to leveraging technology to promote transparency and improve public services delivery remains a significant focus, and the government has been actively using e-government to modernize its public services, improve transparency and enhance efficiency. Rwanda's e-government efforts have been part of a broader vision to transform the country into a knowledge-based economy and improve the overall quality of life of its citizens, and it continues to work toward enhancing their e-government offerings and infrastructure.

South Korea

South Korea has been a pioneer in the implementation of e-government initiatives aiming to enhance public services, improve efficiency, and promote transparency. Its success can be attributed to its strong commitment to digital innovation, strategic planning, and a focus on delivering efficient and user-centric public services. The government continues to invest in and expand its e-government offerings to meet the evolving needs of its citizens and businesses.

United Arab Emirates (UAE)

The UAE's commitment to digital innovation and its efforts to create a smart and efficient government have led to the successful implementation of various e-government services, to enhance public services, improve government efficiency, and promote innovation. These initiatives are intended to enhance the quality of life for residents and promote economic growth in the region.

Uruguay

Uruguay's e-government initiatives were aimed at simplifying interaction between citizens and the government while promoting the use of digital technologies to drive economic and social development. Efforts focused on increasing accessibility, improve efficiency, and enhance transparency in the delivery of public services.

The range of services a government may offer is quite broad, and this depends on their context, the status of development in e-government services and initiatives. Names given to the services offered may also differ from country to country, often in order for them to make more sense to a particular context or culture. Services themselves may range from the most basic, like a digital signature, to more advanced services, like access to digital police services or even digital voting. Table 1 provides a comprehensive list of services that may be offered.

Maintaining a high level of service is essential, and governments need to consider which services to include in their portfolio, for example interoperability, integrated data centers, user-centric design, and provision of open data (available in machine readable format). To instill citizen trust in e-government, it needs to have robust data security and privacy protection, enshrined in a solid legal and regulatory framework. Since not all citizens may have the necessary digital skills to use e-government services, outreach and training providing literacy programs to the general public are strongly encouraged, not least in order to ensure digital inclusion for everyone.

Digital services are prone to change and thus governments need to ensure that any programs designed are scalable and include future-readiness. For e-government services to be sustainable, it may be necessary to engage in public–private partnerships (PPPs), and partnerships with international organizations, which may aid on a national or regional level.

Additional services which may also improve efficiency and effectiveness are the so-called government e-Marketplace and e-Procurement platforms. Smart City projects, housing digital providers in one area, have proven effective and beneficial due to the dynamics and spirit of cooperation they may create among providers.

Any digitalization program needs to remain alert and open to improvements, thus providers need to create feedback mechanisms where users can give suggestions on how services are perceived and can be improved. Irrespective of the feedback for improvement it may receive, providers themselves need to introduce quality control mechanisms, including program evaluation and measurements for efficiency and effectiveness. These measures would give reassurance and encourage citizens to use the services.

Risk Management

Countries that implement e-government initiatives understand that risk management is crucial and by adopting a holistic approach they can minimize dangers and provide users with safe and secure e-government services. Regular updates and collaboration with cybersecurity experts, as well as international organizations can further strengthen a country's e-government security posture. There are numerous risk management issues to address. First are *cybersecurity measures* including protection from cyber threats, including malware, phishing, and distributed denial-of-service (DDoS) attacks; regularly updating and patching software and systems as well as conducting security audits and penetration testing to identify and reduce security weaknesses. Second, e-government risk management should involve the *encryption of sensitive data* at all points to protect it from unauthorized access as well as use strong encryption protocols and secure communication channels. Third, risk management should consider the use of *access control mechanisms* to restrict system access to authorized personnel only, in addition to the use of multi-factor authentication (MFA) to verify the identity of users. This also requires continuous and transparent monitoring of e-government usage. Fourth, e-government should institute *data privacy laws and regulations* to protect user personal information. Fifth, risk management requires *regular audits and assessments* and use the audit results to improve security measures and practices. Sixth, e-government should develop and maintain *incident response plans* to address security and data breaches promptly. Seventh, e-government risk management requires *investments in educating government employees* and users about cybersecurity best practices, comprising recognizing and reporting security threats. Lastly, e-government risk management practices should be *compliant with international best-practices and standards* which could include adherence with international standards and best practices for cybersecurity and data protection, such as ISO 27001 or NIST Cybersecurity Framework.

Role of Organizational and Bureaucratic Culture in the Development of e-Government

Since culture shapes how government agencies operate, make decisions, and interact with citizens and other stakeholders, the organizational and bureaucratic culture within government agencies significantly influences the development, implementation, and success of e-government initiatives. Cultures that embrace innovation, customer-centricity, collaboration, transparency, and ethical considerations are more likely to facilitate effective deployment of e-government solutions that meet the needs of citizens and enhance government services. Recognizing and addressing these cultural factors is essential for the long-term success of e-government projects. Some key organizational and bureaucratic characteristics necessary for e-government development are as follows: First, culture within government agencies can either foster or hinder innovation. Agencies with a *culture that values innovation* are more likely to embrace new technologies and e-government solutions. Second, government agencies that are *customer-focused*, prioritizing customer satisfaction and service delivery are more likely to design user-friendly interfaces, streamline processes, and respond to citizen feedback. Third, a culture of *cooperation and interagency coordination* facilitates the integration of services and data sharing across government departments, leading to more efficient and integrated e-government solutions. Fourth, an e-government culture that values *data and evidence-based decision-making* can lead to the development of data analytics and reporting capabilities within government agencies. This, in turn, enables better policy formulation and program evaluation in the context of e-government. Fifth, a culture of *transparency and accountability* is crucial for building trust with citizens, and Agencies that prioritize transparency are more likely to make government data and decision-making processes accessible to the public. Sixth, an *organizational culture that embraces change* is essential for the successful implementation of e-government initiatives. Change-resistant cultures can impede the adoption of new technologies and processes. Seventh, cultures that prioritize *continuous learning and skills development* are more likely to have employees who can effectively use and manage e-government systems.

Furthermore, organizational behavior and structure impact the success of e-government initiatives and strategies. First, *leadership* within government agencies plays a pivotal role in shaping organizational culture. Leaders who champion e-government and set the tone for innovation and efficiency can drive successful digital transformation efforts. Second, in government bureaucracies, silos can hinder data sharing and collaboration. A culture that discourages siloed thinking and *encourages cross-functional teams* can facilitate the development of integrated e-government services. Third, an organization that values *ethical conduct* can lead to better protection of user data, including privacy and security. Lastly, organizations that are *flexible and adaptive* can respond more effectively to the dynamic environment, changing technologies and user needs of e-Government.

Current and Emerging Trends in e-Government

E-government is also evolving across several key trends through Blockchain, Artificial Intelligence and Quantum Computing. For example, Blockchain is enhancing security, transparency, and efficiency in transactions and records, since its technology ensures secure, immutable records, reducing the risk of fraud and tampering in government transactions. Blockchain also offers transparency and accountability since public ledgers provide transparency, allowing citizens to trace transactions which enhances accountability. These are especially important for applications such as digital identity, voting systems, land and property records, public procurement as well as healthcare records. Estonia and Dubai are regarded as pioneers in using blockchain for e-government.

Artificial Intelligence (AI) is transforming many areas of e-government beyond more automation. AI has enhanced decision-making due to data-driven policies and better identification and mitigation of risks, such as fraud detection and crisis management. Public services have also improved due to more personalized services and smart infrastructure, contributing to enhanced citizen engagement, assisted via chatbots and virtual assistants. AI optimizes workflows and resource management, contributing to operational efficiency and cost reduction. It has become a useful tool in providing AI-informed economic policies and support for startups. AI is considered pivotal for an ethical and inclusive governance, ensuring fair decision-making via bias detection and ensuring accessibility through assistive and inclusive policies. It can be further developed for AI-driven insights for public sector research. Countries with experience using AI in e-government include Singapore (traffic management, public safety, and efficient service delivery through its Smart Nation initiative); The USA (healthcare administration, fraud detection, and improving veterans' services); and Canada (predictive analytics in public health, improving the efficiency of social services, and managing public resources).

Quantum Computing holds promise for an improved e-government in several areas. These include enhanced, faster and larger data processing via Big Data Analytics and complex modeling which enables simulations for socioeconomic and environmental issues. Quantum Encryption is helpful for creating unbreakable security for communication and transactions and expands cybersecurity through advanced pattern analysis. The optimization of public resources is improved via better resource management and supply chain optimization, especially in case of disaster relief.

Quantum Computing is critical for advanced simulation and modeling through detailed scenario planning as well as climate modeling, which improves predictions and disaster preparedness. Quantum Computing can also contribute to innovation and research in medicine and material sciences, via personalized medicine and drug discovery.

All these can also improve ethical and regulatory considerations, especially data privacy, transparency and accountability. Notable countries advancing national capabilities in quantum technology include the USA, whose government is investing in quantum computing research through initiatives like the National Quantum Initiative; the European Union, where its Quantum Flagship program is funding research and development in quantum technologies, including potential applications for e-government; and China, which is also investing heavily in quantum research, making significant advancements in quantum communication and computing, potentially influencing its e-government strategies.

Conclusion

It can safely be said that e-government nowadays is being used in all continents of the world. This section has looked at some of the e-government models currently in use, as well as some future trends. Services range from the very basic, for example simple digital id services, to well advanced in many others, as access to digital police services or the judiciary, or even digital voting.

The section has looked in detail into all aspects of "by-design principles," including digital by design, open or private by design, and automated by design. The section also looked at the necessary key criteria that governments need for them to introduce and implement e-government services, where future scalability and feedback mechanisms play a crucial role.

Digital services need to be designed with the user in mind. They need to be readily available and user-friendly. However, they also need to be safe, thus the role of risk and how it should be managed is considered crucial for e-government services.

5 Digitization of Government Services: Accountability, Efficiency, and Democracy

The rising advancement of digital technologies has changed how governments engage with citizens. The United Nations Division for Public Institutions and Digital Government (n.d.) officially defines e-government as "the use of ICTs to more effectively and efficiently deliver government services to citizens and businesses" (para. 4). Common examples of government services that can be digitized include registering births, getting a driver's license, paying taxes, applying for welfare services and subsidies, and applying for business permits. E-government services first emerged in the late 1990s in developed economies such as the US and have been on the rise ever since, spreading in recent years to emerging economies such as those in South America, Africa, the Middle East, and Asia (Vîlceanu, 2022). The transition from pen and paper to computer and data represents not only a change in the format of government services but an entire reconfiguration of the relationship between citizen and state and the expectations of either party toward the other (Krishna, 2021).

Citizens in emerging economies face many difficulties when accessing government services, ranging from corruption and bureaucracy in governance structures to infrastructure barriers that prevent easy transport to physical government offices (Paul et al., 2020). With nations in this category hosting most of the world's populations and steadily taking up more significant roles on the global political and economic stage, their e-government initiatives must be accessible, transparent, and democratic (Martínez Euklidiadas, 2021). Sufficient investment in digital technologies across all public administration realms can help drive development with other forces, such as increased mobile connectivity, expanding middle classes, and rapid urbanization. The COVID-19 pandemic was a turning point in recognizing the importance of digital infrastructure in public life, the robustness of which determined whether essential services could continue in times of crisis (Wandaogo, 2022).

The digitization of government services can potentially be a transformative force in emerging economies. However, implementing such services is not without challenges and barriers, nor is any technology ideologically neutral when in the hands of governments, especially authoritarian or transitioning regimes (Siqueira et al., 2023). This section reviews the key benefits and challenges of implementing e-government in emerging economies, with recommendations for implementing these platforms to ensure maximum positive impact and inclusivity.

How e-Government Enhances the Quality and Experience of Citizen Interactions with Government

There are many accessibility issues that citizens in emerging economies face in accessing government services (Mustaf et al., 2020). Geographical and infrastructure barriers are among the most prominent. With many emerging economies having poor infrastructure and transport services, as well as sizeable rural populations, it could prove challenging for a citizen to visit a government office in person when they are faced with unreliable or nonexistent public transport, coupled with long distances between, for example, rural villages and city centers where public offices might be (Matthess & Kunkel, 2020).

Language and education barriers are another common hurdle. Emerging economies tend to have ethnically diverse populations that may consist of many indigenous or immigrant groups (Bhagat et al., 2022). Additionally, many emerging economies have high levels of citizens who are illiterate or have received little or no formal education. Thus, citizens who do not speak, or do not have a high level of fluency in the central government language, are illiterate, or are uneducated are disadvantaged in understanding government procedures and forms or speaking to government officials (Paul et al., 2020). Women are additionally disadvantaged in this context, as they are more likely to lack education or literacy in emerging economies and have fewer opportunities to leave their homes and travel to access government services (Malik, 2022).

E-government bridges this accessibility divide by making government services available 24/7 to citizens with an internet connection and a computer or mobile device (Ali, 2020). Citizens can access these platforms whenever they want, without adhering to traditional working hours, travel long distances, or leave their homes. This availability can even out rural residents and women's disadvantages in accessing these services (Paul et al., 2020). The design of e-government platforms is crucial in ensuring they are accessible to citizens with low education, literacy, and/or technical skills. In this respect, the most effective platforms are the ones that are easy to understand and navigate and free of jargon and advanced language, with auto-translate programs or multiple language options to accommodate citizens from diverse ethnic and indigenous groups (Upadhyay et al., 2022).

With regards to accessibility, these platforms can also potentially remove the barriers that disabled or impaired citizens face in accessing government services (Matthess & Kunkel, 2020). In addition to transportation and distance difficulties, disabled citizens or those who are hearing or vision impaired, such as older adults, are doubly disadvantaged in accessing government services (Upadhyay et al., 2022). E-government platforms that include voice commands, screen readers, alternative texts, and other web accessibility measures can cross this divide and give disabled citizens previously inconceivable access to government services (Bhagat et al., 2022).

India is one example where e-government has improved the accessibility of government services. As of 2021, 65% of the Indian population lives in rural areas, and the country faces frequent problems with poor infrastructure and public transport (PIB Delhi, 2023). In addition, the country has over two thousand ethnic groups and 122 major languages (Encyclopedia Britannica, n.d.; Hartley, 2021). In 2015, the government of India launched Digital India, a program to improve digital infrastructure and utility, make public services available digitally, and improve citizens' digital literacy (Dar & Nagrath, 2022). The program included the launch of various e-government platforms. The leading platforms created under this program include the Unified Mobile

Application for New-age Governance (UMANG), a mobile app that provides access to numerous government services; DigiLocker, a platform that issues and verifies official documents and certificates; Jeevan Pramaan, a digital life certificate for pensioners; and National Scholarships Portal, which allows students to apply for scholarship schemes provided by the Indian government (Government of India, n.d.).

In addition to accessibility requirements, e-government has vast potential to transform the bureaucracy and corruption rife in emerging economies' public services (Pamungkas et al., 2023). Bribery is one of the most common forms of corruption citizens in emerging economies face when accessing public services. It is a common practice for officials to demand bribes for services that should be free or to expedite traditionally time-consuming services (Organisation for Economic Co-operation and Development Center [OECDDC], 2022). This practice is especially prevalent when there is a lack of transparency and excessive discretionary power in governments, which is common in emerging economies. Nepotism also follows, with officials prioritizing services given to their connections, or citizens with the "right" political loyalty, leaving those on the opposite side of the coin receiving delayed or inferior services (Lemieux, 2016).

Excessive bureaucracy and delays are also commonplace in public services in emerging economies. Often, standard public services involve unnecessarily complex procedures and red tape, such as applying for a business or building permit (Vîlceanu, 2022). Poor management, lack of funds or misallocation, lack of accountability, and poor infrastructure can also lead to delays and inefficiency in public services (Mustaf et al., 2020). Political instability and conflict can add to this burden, leading to corruption or the complete stopping of public services (Mustaf et al., 2020).

E-government has the potential to reduce or altogether remove these barriers. Digitizing services can lead to quicker, more efficient delivery, removing the need for multiple human public servants as mediators who may also demand bribes or be nepotistic in their interactions with citizens (Lemieux, 2016). The digitization of these transactions also leaves a more transparent audit trail, making corruption easier to detect and ultimately reducing it while standardizing services for every citizen. E-government can also be cheaper to implement and manage than in-person services, mitigating the adverse effects of lack of funding on public service processes (Valle-Cruz, 2019). Additionally, e-government platforms usually incorporate feedback mechanisms and collect advanced data analytics, allowing governments to identify inefficiencies or flaws in the system and correct them (Al-Besher & Kumar, 2022).

One example of e-governance that successfully mitigates corruption and bureaucracy is NADRA (The National Database and Registration Authority) in Pakistan. Founded in 2000, the authority uses smart national identity cards that contain data chips and biometric data, all integrated into one digital national identity database (Malik, 2022). NADRA also offers digitized public services, such as registering marriages, births, and deaths, and linking their systems with other public authorities, such as the Directorate General of Immigration & Passports, to streamline the issuing of passports (Rehman et al., 2018). The digital identity database and biometric-based identity cards have significantly reduced voter fraud and identity fraud in claiming welfare benefits (Malik, 2022). This digital identity system has also made financial services more accessible and a critical tool in counter-terrorism efforts (Malik, 2022).

The Dark Side of Digitization: Digital Surveillance and Citizen Trust in Government

Although the digitization of government services and the implementation of e-government have many benefits, it also has noted downsides that have been explored in-depth in the literature. The chief concerns in this regard are the surveillance of citizens and the erosion of citizens' privacy and trust in government (Pamungkas et al., 2023). The more citizens' private data is stored online or in digital databases, the greater the risk of this data being hacked or illegally accessed by government agencies (Yeniceler & Ilgın, 2019). The increasing digitization of government services can also lead to more opportunities for illegal surveillance of citizens by government and intelligence forces. This surveillance can include using facial recognition technologies and tracking citizens' personal online communications and social media activities (Bayaga & Ophoff, 2019). Although some level of surveillance on certain citizens of interest is necessary for national security, there is a significant risk of this surveillance extending to greater numbers of the population and crossing ethical quandaries between security requirements and authoritarian control (Bayaga & Ophoff, 2019).

These issues are exacerbated when no legal or regulatory frameworks are in place for how to use citizens' personal data or regulate surveillance efforts. There needs to be more regulation for how emerging technologies are used in these efforts, such as AI systems used in facial recognition technology or in spying on specific persons or populations (Al-Besher & Kumar, 2022). Additionally, transparency in how governments use citizen data may make citizens afraid to express political opinions or participate in political actions, lest they are unjustly targeted (Valle-Cruz, 2019).

These concerns are exacerbated in emerging economies, where technology uptake and democratic institutions may be weak or still in early emergent stages. Many emerging economies are rapidly adopting digital and emerging technologies such as AI for government use (Al-Besher & Kumar, 2022). However, this is done with insufficient regulations in place or with inadequate oversight, given that emerging economies often face the issues of a lack of transparency and accountability in government in general (OECDDC, 2022). Weak or transitional democratic institutions in emerging economies may also lead to a misuse of these technologies to stifle political opposition, dissent, manipulate election outcomes, or other results of democratic processes (Siqueira et al., 2023). The lack of regulatory frameworks in emerging economies applies to digital surveillance and more routine data protection laws, which leaves citizens' data vulnerable to public and corporate misuse (Shah et al., 2022).

Infrastructure weaknesses and concerns also leave citizens' data vulnerable to misuse. Emerging economies sometimes lack comprehensive cybersecurity infrastructures, increasing the risk of mass data breaches (Mishra et al., 2021). Digital divides, and a lack of digital literacy among specific populations in emerging economies also leave many citizens disadvantaged in protecting their privacy and avoiding surveillance. This lack of awareness is increased when governments purposefully hide information about data misuse and surveillance, leaving the general public unaware of how much their data is being used (Shah et al., 2022). Since many emerging economies exhibit collectivistic cultures, governments may use collectivistic cultural norms about authority or individual rights to conduct surveillance activities (Mustaf et al., 2020). Governments' oppression of civil society and the media, which has often been recorded in emerging economies, may further clear the way for them to conduct illegal and/or unethical surveillance activities (Matthess & Kunkel, 2020).

Government surveillance and data misuse in emerging economies also interact with international forces and interests (Jansen et al., 2023). Governments in emerging economies may feel geopolitical pressures or face economic dependencies in which they must adopt surveillance technologies from more developed nations. Emerging economies' reliance on foreign technologies may also raise concerns about data siphoning or international espionage (Grinin et al., 2022). Conversely, using surveillance technologies in emerging economies may also result in them facing economic or political sanctions from more developed nations, which can deter their economic development and ability to participate in international markets (Jansen et al., 2023).

In one recent example, the Digital India program is anchored around the Aadhaar number, a twelve-digit unique biometric identification number given to every citizen serving as proof of identity and address (Singh, 2021). Cybersecurity concerns have plagued the Aadhaar number in recent years. In

2018, then chairman of the Telecom Regulatory Authority of India, RS Sharma, revealed his Aadhaar number on Twitter, challenging users to expose his personal information from the number alone (Agencies, 2018). Twitter users quickly gathered and posted his mobile number and the make of the phone it was connected to, as well as his email ID, alternative phone number, and email security question. However, other users pointed out that some of this information was in the public domain and thus did not necessarily point to vulnerabilities in the Aadhaar numbers, with the government claiming the same (Agencies, 2018; Sharma, 2018).

In 2022, the Government of India launched a program inviting white hat hackers to expose vulnerabilities in its Central Identities Data Repository containing Aadhaar data (Thathoo, 2022). Nevertheless, in October 2023, a report by private US cybersecurity firm Resecurity revealed that the personal information and Aadhaar numbers of millions of Indian citizens were put up for sale on the dark web, including the fields of name, father's name, phone number, passport and Aadhaar numbers, age, gender, address, district, pin code, and state (Resecurity, 2023). This massive leak leaves citizens vulnerable to e-tax refund fraud and online banking theft (Resecurity, 2023).

This leak coincides with India's stance on the international stage as one of the world's fastest-growing economies with an expanding middle class and enhanced earning power, bank access, and mobile connectivity (Resecurity, 2023). This growth places India as a regional rival to China, leading to the former being the subject of strengthened security and economic relations with the US (Markey & Scobell, 2023). Resecurity (2023) also claims that growing unrest in the Middle East leads to increased cyberattacks, with compromised data being sold online.

The leak also reveals cybersecurity vulnerabilities in these digital government services. Private Indian businesses are already facing a significant increase in cyberattacks, especially ransomware attacks (Sabharwal & Sharma, 2020). A lack of accountability and transparency in these digital systems leads to a further shadowing of how these attacks affect citizens' data, with official government sources frequently claiming the strong security of the Aadhaar system (Sharma, 2018).

Considering the case of the Aadhaar system, it is crucial to note that developing economies are not the only ones to face cybersecurity concerns or hacks of personal data from government sources. These hacks remain a persistent problem globally that calls for increased security of government data systems (Krishna & MP, 2021). For example, in June 2023, millions of citizens of Louisiana and Oregon had their personal data hacked from US government databases by hackers who found their way into the networks from a flaw in a popular file transfer software (Lyngaas, 2023).

Nevertheless, in some cases, it is not cybercriminals but governments using citizens' personal data, especially in citizen surveillance. Perhaps the most notorious example is China's Social Credit system, which combines citizens' employment history, online shopping data, financial records, and social media activity to generate a social credit score for every citizen (Creemers, 2018). Citizens with higher scores will gain access to certain privileges, such as expedited visas, while those with low scores will lose certain rights, such as taking out loans, renting a car, or even finding a job (Chen et al., 2023). The system is being tested through pilot projects at local governments and private companies (Xu et al., 2022).

In a notable example of how international relations affect the surveillance efforts of emerging economies, in 2018, it was reported that the Venezuelan government had contracted Chinese company ZTE to develop a national biometric identification system (Rendon & Kohan, 2019). The result was an identification card system called the Carnet de la Patria or Fatherland Card, which captures citizens' personal data and acts as a digital wallet combined with a personalized QR code. The card was promoted as a voluntary way for citizens to gain greater access to public services; to get a card, citizens first had to answer questions about their economic and social status (Vidal, 2018). About 70% of Venezuelans were issued the card in its first year alone (Vidal, 2018).

The card was made mandatory for citizens to access social services that provide food, medicine, government bonds, gasoline discounts, personal and legal documents (which are notoriously difficult to obtain in Venezuela), and pension payments (Global Voices Online, 2018) (Penfold, 2018; Vidal, 2018). However, many have claimed that the card is used for state control and surveillance. During the 2017 and 2018 elections, it was claimed that citizens were pressured or coerced into not being allowed to vote unless they obtained a card (Vidal, 2018). During the COVID-19 pandemic, other reports claimed that only citizens with a card could have the much-needed COVID-19 vaccines (Yapur & Vasquez, 2021).

Conclusions and Recommendations

Emerging economies are continuing to embrace the digitization of government services. This transition can prove valuable in emerging economies' economic growth, increasing citizens' inclusion and a nation's ability to participate in the economic and political spheres on a global scale (Ranchordás, 2022). However, without adequate oversight and a strategic approach to digitization processes, the digitization of government services will fail to achieve their development goals and instead perpetuate the inefficiency, bureaucracy, corruption, and authoritarianism that so often plagues governments in these economies (Vyas-Doorgapersad, 2022).

In order to mitigate this negative potential, governments should follow a set of recommendations supported by research and practice. Firstly, regulatory frameworks should be implemented to support these digitization processes (OECDDC, 2019). Regulating digitization can prove challenging since the needed technologies can span multiple regulatory regimes and necessitate more cross-border transactions and flows (OECDDC, 2022).

This challenge requires a new approach to communication, coherence, and collaboration among multiple government bodies and external stakeholders (Martínez Euklidiadas, 2021). Given that this unique form of regulation also requires technical expertise and knowledge, governments will need to consult with international regulatory bodies, think tanks, and other institutions in order to ensure they are moving forward with up-to-date knowledge of the risks and benefits of digital technologies and digitization processes (Cenderello & Bertrand, 2022). This process offers unique opportunities for collaboration among the private, public, and third sectors.

One crucial element of these frameworks is data protection laws that include details about citizens' data rights, the obligations of data handlers, and the limits of citizen data used for commercial and surveillance purposes (OECDDC, 2022). These regulations should include enforcement mechanisms such as penalties for violations, which will help deter data misuse. Surveillance is a crucial area in this regard. Governments must clearly define the limits of necessary surveillance, such as in cases of terrorism or national emergencies (Yeniceler & Ilgın, 2019).

Emerging economies can follow best practices from other regions, such as the EU GDPR laws. However, it is crucial not to directly copy regulatory practices from other regions, which can reinforce a colonial mindset in regulation, but instead adapt them to the unique needs, concerns, and preferences of the citizens of the emerging economy in question (Krishna & Sebastian, 2021). These considerations should include promoting data and digital literacies among rural, illiterate, minority, refugee, and/or indigenous populations and how these regulations will be enforced locally, such as through district governance or village councils (Paksi et al., 2022).

Once regulations are in place, their principles should be implemented throughout the design and piloting of e-government platforms (Grinin et al., 2022). Data protection and privacy is crucial in this regard. Developers should have a pre-ordained plan to use only minimal and necessary personal data from citizens for specific purposes, with robust encryption so data in transit and at rest is sufficiently protected (Bayaga & Ophoff, 2019). These platforms should disclose to users at the outset how their data is used and provide opt-out options for citizens who want to limit how their data is used and stored (Shah et al., 2022).

On top of regulatory and ethics concerns, having a solid cybersecurity infrastructure is one of the most crucial considerations when digitizing government services (Ahmet & Kazdal, 2019). A national cybersecurity plan and strategy should be implemented, including intermittent security audits, secure data storage, crisis management plans, and specialized teams for data breaches (Shah et al., 2022). Partnerships with international cybersecurity entities are invaluable in developing such plans and strategies (OECDDC, 2022).

Finally, governments should invest in awareness-raising and digital literacy efforts among their citizen populations (Chohan & Hu, 2022). Advertising and public relations campaigns can spread awareness of e-government platforms, explain how they work, and emphasize the benefits of accessing government services electronically (Bojang, 2019). Training sessions in schools, community centers, village councils, and other public places can also help engage the public at the grassroots level. These public sessions can also include input and feedback mechanisms for citizens to explain their needs and voice their opinions regarding government services (Lytras & Şerban, 2020). This feedback can be vital in ensuring the success of e-government platforms because they ensure that they will have long-term use and become the go-to source for citizens' interactions with the government (Lytras & Şerban, 2020).

The digitization of government services in emerging economies can drive economic growth and development and enhance citizens' trust in and broader relationships with the government (Vyas-Doorgapersad, 2022). However, successful digitization is not a one-off but a long and multifaceted process that involves attention to various areas of governance, from regulation to civic processes to practical concerns around technology use (Mustaf et al., 2020). Emerging economies that succeed will emerge as key players on the global governance stage and serve as models for other emerging economies on the rise (Paul et al., 2020).

6 Conclusion

In emerging economies, governance reform and economic growth are pushed forward by digitalization in the public sector (EMnet Working Group on Digital Transformation in Emerging Markets [EWGDTEM], 2022). Government services are expected to be revolutionized regarding accessibility, efficiency, and transparency when public services become one with digital technologies. Nevertheless, many roadblocks and challenges stand in the way of implementing fully digitalized government services in these economies. Socioeconomic, infrastructural, and institutional constraints are the roots of these significant roadblocks (Organisation for Economic Co-operation and Development [OECD], 2021).

Infrastructure remains one of the primary impediments to implementing digitalization plans in emerging economies (Mustaf et al., 2020). Any digitalization initiative necessitates a robust and reliable internet connection and the appropriate hardware and software, as well as data centers to provide computing power and a high rate of digital device penetration in the general population. Emerging economies lack this needed infrastructure and resources, often relying on developed economies' aid or funding models such as PPPs (World Economic Forum & FTI Consulting, 2023). Nevertheless, beyond infrastructural concerns, sociocultural and political challenges remain equally salient roadblocks to implementing digitalization in the public sector in emerging economies. Resistance to change remains among the most profound issues regarding citizens' mindsets and institutional structures within governments and public sector organizations (Dakduk et al., 2023).

Citizens accustomed to dealing with public services through face-to-face interactions will likely not trust digital solutions initially, especially if their local culture values face-to-face interactions, empathy, and physical touch. Digital technologies may also be seen as threatening traditional ways of life or as imposing values and ideas from developed nations (Yavwa & Twinomurinzi, 2021). In the political realm, politicians or public sector officials may resist digitalization because it clashes with traditional institutional and governance structures, which may be cumbersome, outdated, and bureaucratic and leave room for corruption and misappropriation of funds (Sadik-Zada et al., 2022). The transparency offered by digital public services can be seen as a threat to these structures, even more so when authoritarian governments are involved, who may see this transparency as threatening the status quo and their grip on power (OECD, 2021). Other political aspects of emerging economies, such as unstable governments, short-term election cycles, civilian uprisings, and armed conflict, impede digitalization efforts, requiring long-term planning and deployment, a stable economy, and peaceful social conditions (Malodia et al., 2021).

These roadblocks disadvantage emerging economies regarding how successful their digitalization initiatives can be, but they are not insurmountable. The public sector is ideal for these nations to begin rolling out digitalization initiatives because it is the first point of contact for most citizens with institutional structures (OECD, 2023). Governance structures can be reformed to be more transparent and efficient, pushing forward innovations in how governments interact with and serve their citizens (Trischler & Westman Trischler, 2022).

While there are [potential] solutions to the persistent funding and infrastructure issues, securing financial capital or support is not enough to surmount the aforementioned sociocultural and political roadblocks (OECD, 2021). An understanding, holistic, and agile mindset is needed to surmount these hurdles in which those in charge of digitalization initiatives take the time and effort to understand the target beneficiaries of these initiatives (Gupta, 2023). These efforts involve understanding the culture, needs, and history of the communities and peoples involved and the governance structures they have traditionally dealt with (OECD, 2023). Once this understanding has been achieved, digitalization initiatives can be tailored to their backgrounds and needs. Examples include involving community leaders in spreading awareness about digital services and integrating them into citizens' pre-existing community and social structures (Bertrand & McQueen, 2023). This approach can be applied to political structures as well. Digitalization projects that need government approval can emphasize quick wins and be rolled out in small, incremental stages that align with short-term political cycles, focusing on economic and reputational gain, not to provoke fear or suspicion (Schlogl & Kim, 2023).

Although emerging economies grapple with the multiple challenges, they are also propelled forward by a demographically youthful population, evolving governance structures, and fast economic growth (Mustaf et al., 2020). At the same time, they are also remarkably diverse in terms of democratization, geopolitics, and unique demographic features (Onsongo, 2023). In addition to understanding their sociocultural and economic environment, it is crucial to understand these economies' institutional landscape and how it affects their policy practices, which can enable or stifle digitalization efforts (Rottig, 2016). Institutional voids remain a critical weakness unique to emerging economies. These voids act as barriers for investors and businesses to operate in these markets, negatively impacting investments and entry barriers (Yildirim et al., 2022). Inadequate financial structures and legal inconsistencies are among these markets' most common voids (Koch, 2022). Digitalization thus presents the opportunity to accelerate economic growth and allow these markets to compete globally (Brieger et al., 2022).

Technology leapfrogging presents a solution to these voids, allowing these markets to adopt advanced technologies and thus bypass conventional development stages (Hensmans, 2023). This process can allow emerging economies to surpass their historical disparities with developed economies, resulting in improved efficiency and significant cost savings for the public sector

(Afawubo & Noglo, 2022). These advanced technologies can include smart city initiatives, mobile government applications, digital identity systems, and e-education initiatives. However, fast-paced growth must be inclusive and sustainable to avoid exacerbating social divides and creating more problems than it solves (Fomba Kamga et al., 2022).

Digital infrastructure projects must aim to make digital technologies and services available to all segments of a nation's population, including ethnic and religious groups, those living in rural locations, and tribal or nomadic groups (Malamud et al., 2019). Institutional capacity must also be strengthened to provide the foundation for inclusive and sustainable digital transformation. Thus, alongside the adoption of digital tools in governments, governance practices need to be reformed from within, as do legal frameworks and regulations that will create the right enabling environment for such technologies to thrive (Satoglu, 2020). Legal and regulatory concerns should also consider cybersecurity and data privacy, citizen participation, and supporting digital entrepreneurship and digital innovation (Koop & Kessler, 2021).

E-government projects are among the first and most effective initiatives for an emerging economy wishing to digitalize its public sector (Bertrand & McQueen, 2023). E-government involves digitalizing government services through initiatives such as digital IDs, centralized public service portals, and electronic services provision. Automation, privacy, and openness principles need to be implemented for e-government projects to be successful and ensure efficient, user-centric, and secure e-government platforms and systems (Cendrello & Bertrand, 2022). These principles are implemented through user-centric design, transparency, efficiency, accessibility, inclusion, regulatory compliance, scalability, interoperability, security, and an agile approach to incorporating user feedback (Di Giulio & Vecchi, 2023).

The cases of e-government explored in this Element from Estonia, India, Rwanda, South Korea, the UAE, and Uruguay demonstrate the importance of these principles and the need to strike a balance between robust regulation and enabling innovation in e-government design and service delivery. Risk management is crucial to ensure that e-government initiatives thrive in light of the many barriers and difficulties emerging economies face (OECD, 2021). E-government tools and platforms and the software and hardware behind them must be ultra-secure through data encryption, privacy compliance, access control, incident response, cybersecurity audits, user education, and continuous improvements through an agile development approach (Onsongo, 2023).

Organizational culture is also crucial to the success of e-government initiatives. Bureaucratic cultures can resist change and the speed and transparency of e-government projects (Vyas-Doorgapersad, 2022). In order to develop successful e-government solutions, the organization behind them must first embrace a mindset of innovation, collaboration, and customer-centricity, seeing the transparency of e-government as an effective means to combat corruption and gain citizen trust (Martínez Euklidiadas, 2021). While designing e-government solutions, an organization with this mindset will embrace cutting-edge technologies while adhering to national and international regulations and actively involve citizens in the development and deployment process. The organization must also embrace change and be ready to implement effective change management practices (Rossidis et al., 2023).

At an organization-wide level, leadership is also crucial to the success of e-government projects. Effective organizational leaders in these situations voice support for the specific project and the broader benefits of digitalization to organizational and societal functioning (Di Giulio & Vecchi, 2023). These leaders embrace innovation and an agile mindset, allowing employees and the public to have an equal voice in developing e-government projects (Krishna & Sebastian, 2021). Leadership must also embrace collaboration and frequently organize collaborative efforts across different government agencies and departments and between the public, private, and third sectors (Hammerschmid et al., 2023). This mindset also extends to data sharing efforts and making information and data about e-government projects open access to various involved stakeholders (Valle-Cruz et al., 2023). Leaders must also embrace and respect ethical guidelines. These efforts include establishing ethics committees, carefully adhering to national and international laws, and emulating best-use cases of digitalization ethics from other nations or public institutions (Heuberger, 2022; Wouters et al., 2023).

In emerging economies, digitalization holds great potential for economic growth, social progress, and national competitiveness (Asian Productivity Organization, 2021). The theories, concepts, and cases explored in this Element have examined the significant challenges and determining success factors that can make or break the digitalization process in emerging economies. Right now, the emerging economies of the world are at a crossroads. Some have already established a presence in business, politics, tech, and culture, while others are poised to shake up the global stage as they grow in economic, cultural, and political influence (Cendrello & Bertrand, 2022).

Digitalization allows these economies to grow exponentially, leapfrogging developmental inequities and joining the world's developed nations toward ever-increasing public sector innovation (Dakduk et al., 2023). Nevertheless, this potential is not without risks or caveats, and any growth must be shepherded around the principles of participatory, inclusive, and sustainable growth (Onsongo, 2023). Governments and public services ideally exist to serve the needs of their citizens, and digitalization is one crucial tool to better serve, protect, and engage citizens (Di Giulio & Vecchi, 2023). Striving toward this ideal benefits emerging economies politically and economically accelerates their development, and puts them on course to an equitable, sustainable future.

To address the challenges discussed in this Element and to harness the opportunities presented by digitalization in emerging economies, several specific policy recommendations can help guide governance reform and accelerate economic growth. We identify seven as follows:

1. Infrastructure Development and PPPs: One of the primary barriers to digital transformation is the lack of robust infrastructure. Governments in emerging economies should allocate investments in critical digital infrastructure, such as high-speed internet access, cloud computing, and data centers. While it shouldn't be the only method, PPPs have a role here, where private companies can contribute capital and expertise while public entities focus on regulation and enabling policies. This may be a sensible risk pooling approach. By leveraging PPPs, countries can efficiently build the digital backbone required for large-scale digitalization projects. Additionally, governments could consider adopting smart cities initiatives that integrate various sectors like healthcare, transport, and education through digital technologies.

2. Tailored Digital Literacy Programs: No amount of infrastructure investment will address the challenges without a commitment to enhancing Digital literacy among society. This is essential to ensure that citizens across different socioeconomic strata can access and effectively use digital services as well as addressing existing digital divides between the digital "haves and have nots." Policymakers should design digital literacy programs specifically tailored to different demographics, particularly those in rural areas, low-income communities, as well as older age groups. These programs should focus on basic digital skills as well as trust-building initiatives to address concerns about privacy, security, and the reliability of digital government services. Special attention should also be given to including ethnic minorities, nomadic groups, and other marginalized communities in these initiatives.

3. Regulatory and Legal Frameworks for Digital Transformation: Alongside physical infrastructure, emerging economies need to build regulatory and legal frameworks to enable the smooth implementation of digital public services. Governments should establish clear policies around data privacy, cybersecurity, and intellectual property rights, ensuring that legal systems are aligned with the needs of digital economies. There are best practices that emerging economies could adopt such as the EU's General Data Protection Regulation (GDPR) as well as relevant elements of other EU legislation embodied in the Digital Services Act and the innovative EU AI Act. At the same time, adopting in full legislation from the EU may cause regulatory rigidities which emerging economies should avoid. Digital policy flexibility is crucial to encourage innovation. For instance, creating regulatory sandboxes could allow governments to test new digital solutions before full-scale implementation, thus fostering innovation while managing risk at the same time.

4. Change Management and Organizational Culture Shift: Challenges in digitalizing government services are commonly associated with institutional dysfunction. Policymakers should push for change management initiatives that focus on reducing resistance to digitalization within government agencies and the key administrators. This could involve transformational executive training of public officials focusing on the benefits of digitalization to government work as well as fostering interest in adopting digital tools. Governments should aim to build a culture of innovation and collaboration among their staff, encouraging the use of digital tools to increase transparency and reduce bureaucracy.

5. Incremental and Context-Specific Implementation: Digitalization efforts in emerging economies should be implemented incrementally, focusing on quick wins that align with short-term political cycles. Policymakers can prioritize the digitalization of specific public services (such as issuing digital IDs, tax filing, or healthcare services) that can demonstrate clear economic or social benefits. Additionally, these digital projects should be tailored to the cultural and political context of each country. Engaging local leaders and stakeholders in the design and implementation process will help ensure that digital services are accepted by the broader population and integrated into existing social structures.

6. Leapfrogging Technologies and Inclusive Growth: Emerging economies have the opportunity to leapfrog traditional developmental stages in digitization by adopting advanced technologies. The rapid growth induced by leapfrogging must also be inclusive (see point 2) to prevent exacerbating existing inequalities. Policymakers should focus on making digital services and infrastructure available to all segments of society, especially those in rural or underserved regions. In parallel, institutional capacity must be strengthened to manage these technologies effectively, ensuring they are used sustainably and equitably.

7. Strengthening Governance and Tackling Corruption: One of the most formidable barriers to successful digital transformation in many emerging economies is the pervasive nature of corruption. The promotion of transparency and rigorous enforcement of integrity and ethics codes through the adoption of digital platforms are an effective means of reducing opportunities for corruption. For example, automating government services and establishing digital audit trails can minimize the chances of fund misappropriation. This doesn't imply that digital transparency is a panacea for corruption as many of the underlying pressures for corruption may persist, however, raising the risks of being caught through digital transparency is likely to reduce the incidence of corrupt acts. Embracing open government initiatives that allow citizens to track public spending and access government data in real-time could further enhance trust in digital governance and legitimacy.

In conclusion, while digital transformation presents numerous challenges, particularly in emerging economies, proper policy responses facilitate inclusive growth, transparency, and improved governance. By focusing on infrastructure, literacy, regulation, and institution-building, emerging economies can leverage digital tools to propel themselves toward sustainable development.

References

Abdullah, P. P., Raharjo, T., Hardian, B., & Simanungkalit, T. (2023). Challenges and best practices solution of agile project management in public sector: A systematic literature review. *JOIV: International Journal on Informatics Visualization*, *7*(2), 606–614. http://dx.doi.org/10.30630/joiv.7.2.1098.

Afawubo, K., & Noglo, Y. A. (2022). ICT and entrepreneurship: A comparative analysis of developing, emerging and developed countries. *Technological Forecasting and Social Change*, *175*, Article 121312. https://doi.org/10.1016/j.techfore.2021.121312.

Agencies. (2018, July 28). TRAI chief's personal details leaked after he shares Aadhaar number in challenge to hackers. *The New Indian Express*. www.newindianexpress.com/nation/2018/jul/28/trai-chiefs-personal-details-leaked-after-he-shares-aadhaar-number-in-challenge-to-hackers-1850002.html.

Agency of Electronic Government and Society of Information and Knowledge (2024). https://observatorioplanificacion.cepal.org/en/institutions/open-government-division-agency-electronic-government-and-information-and-knowledge.

Ahmet, E. F. E., & Kazdal, H. (2019). It security trends for e-government threats. *International Journal of Multidisciplinary Studies and Innovative Technologies*, *3*(2), 105–110.

Al-Besher, A., & Kumar, K. (2022). Use of artificial intelligence to enhance e-government services. *Measurement: Sensors*, *24*, 100484.

Ali, D. M. M. (2020). Digitization of the emerging economy: An exploratory and explanatory case study. *Journal of Governance and Regulation*, *9*(4), 25–36.

Allmann, K., & Radu, R. (2023). Digital footprints as barriers to accessing e-government services. *Global Policy*, *14*(1), 84–94. https://doi.org/10.1111/1758-5899.13140.

Ameen, K., & Gorman, G.E. (2009) Information and digital literacy: A stumbling block to development? A Pakistan perspective. *Library Management*, *30*(1–2), 99–112.

Apolitical. (2017, March 20). *Mexico bridges digital divide with internet cafes in poor areas.* https://apolitical.co/solution-articles/en/mexico-bridges-digital-divide-internet-cafes-poor-areas.

Arnold, D. J., & Quelch, J. A. (1998). New strategies in emerging markets. *MIT Sloan Management Review*, *40*(1), 7–20.

Asian Productivity Organization. (2021). *Digitalization of public service delivery in Asia*. www.apo-tokyo.org/wp-content/uploads/2021/02/Digitalization-of-Public-Service-Delivery-in-Asia-final-1.pdf.

Bayaga, A., & Ophoff, J. (2019, September). Determinants of e-government use in developing countries: the influence of privacy and security concerns. In A. Bayaga & J. Ophoff (Eds.), *2019 Conference on Next Generation Computing Applications (NextComp)* (pp. 1–7). IEEE.

Bertrand, A., & McQueen, J. (2023, June 19). *How can digital government connect citizens without leaving the disconnected behind?* Ernst & Young. www.ey.com/en_gr/government-public-sector/how-can-digital-government-connect-citizens-without-leaving-the-disconnected-behind.

Bhagat, C., Mishra, A. K., & Aithal, P. S. (2022). Model for implementation of e-Government services in developing countries like Nepal. *International Journal of Case Studies in Business, IT and Education (IJCSBE), 6*(2), 320–333.

Bojang, M. B. (2019). Challenges and successes of e-Government development in developing countries: A theoretical review of the literature. *International Journal of Research and Innovation in Social Science, 3*(4), 410–414.

Brieger, S. A., Chowdhury, F., Hechavarría, D. M., et al. (2022). Digitalization, institutions and new venture internationalization. *Journal of International Management, 28*(4), Article 100949. https://doi.org/10.1016/j.intman.2022.100949.

Broadman H. G., Anderson J., Claessens C. A., et al. (2004). *Building market institutions in South Eastern Europe: Comparative prospects for investment and private sector development*. The World Bank.

Cavusgil, S. T., Deligonul, S., Kardes, I., & Cavusgil, E. (2018). Middle-class consumers in emerging markets: Conceptualization, propositions, and implications for international marketers. *Journal of International Marketing, 26*(3), 94–108.

Cendrello, A., & Bertrand, A. (2022, October 4). *How governments in developing countries can close the digital divide*. Ernst & Young. www.ey.com/en_gl/international-development/how-governments-in-developing-countries-can-close-the-digital-gap.

Chen, M., Engelmann, S., & Grossklags, J. (2023). Social credit system and privacy. In S. Trepte & P. Masur (Eds.), *The Routledge handbook of privacy and social media* (pp. 227–236). Routledge.

Chohan, S. R., & Hu, G. (2022). Strengthening digital inclusion through e-government: Cohesive ICT training programs to intensify digital competency. *Information Technology for Development, 28*(1), 16–38.

Ciancarini, P., Giancarlo, R., & Grimaudo, G. (2024). Scrum@ PA: Tailoring an agile methodology to the digital transformation in the public sector. *Information*, *15*(2), Article 110. https://doi.org/10.3390/info15020110.

Creemers, R. (2018). China's social credit system: An evolving practice of control. *SSRN Electronic Journal*. http://dx.doi.org/10.2139/ssrn.3175792.

da Silva, L. F., Zitkus, E., & Freire, A. P. (2023). An exploratory study of the use of the internet and e-government by older adults in the countryside of Brazil. *Information*, *14*(4), Article 225. https://doi.org/10.3390/info14040225.

Dakduk, S., Van der Woude, D., & Nieto, C. A. (2023). Technological adoption in emerging economies: Insights from Latin America and the Caribbean with a focus on low-income consumers. In V. Bobek & T. Horvat (Eds.), *New topics in emerging markets* (pp. 1–24). IntechOpen. http://dx.doi.org/10.5772/intechopen.112004.

Dar, S. A., & Nagrath, D. (2022). Digital India: Where knowledge is strength and empowers the people. *International Journal of Educational Review, Law and Social Sciences (IJERLAS)*, *2*(3), 437–446. https://doi.org/10.54443/ijerlas.v2i3.274.

Dawes, S. S., & Cresswell, A. M. (2012). Antecedents of perceived benefits of electronic government: An empirical examination. *Public Administration Review*, *72*(3), 413–427.

Di Giulio, M., & Vecchi, G. (2023). Implementing digitalization in the public sector. Technologies, agency, and governance. *Public Policy and Administration*, *38*(2), 133–158. https://doi.org/10.1177/09520767211023283.

Digital India. (n.d.). *Home*. Retrieved November 9, 2023, from https://digitalindia.gov.in.

Encyclopedia Britannica. (n.d.). *People of India*. Retrieved November 10, 2023, from www.britannica.com/place/India/People.

Dwivedi, Y. K., Wastell, D., Laumer, S., et al. (2015). Research on information systems failures and successes: Status update and future directions. Information Systems Frontiers, *17*(1), 143–157.

Edelmann, N., Mergel, I., & Lampoltshammer, T. (2023). Competences that foster digital transformation of public administrations: An Austrian case study. *Administrative Sciences*, *13*(2), Article 44. https://doi.org/10.3390/admsci13020044v

E-Government in South Korea (2024). Statistics and Facts, www.statista.com/topics/8246/e-government-in-south-korea/#topicOverview.

Elam, A. (2023). Human computer interaction (HCI) as a key constraint in the e-government and digitalization of Afghanistan. *Technium Social Sciences Journal*, *39*(1), 220–233. https://doi.org/10.47577/tssj.v39i1.8115.

EMnet Working Group on Digital Transformation in Emerging Markets. (2022). *The future of digital transformation in emerging markets.* Organisation for Economic Co-operation and Development. www.oecd.org/dev/Key_ Messages_EMnet_WorkingGroup_DigitalTransformation_EmergingMarkets .pdf.

Enaifoghe, A., Dlamini, N. P., Jili, N. N., & Mthethwa, R. (2023). The role of e-government as enabler of good governance for socio-economic development in South Africa. *International Journal of Social Science Research and Review, 6*(1), 493–508. https://doi.org/10.47814/ijssrr.v6i1.826.

Encyclopedia Britannica. (n.d.). *People of India.* Retrieved February 1, 2024, from www.britannica.com/place/India/People.

Engvall, T., & Flak, L. S. (2022). Digital governance as a scientific concept. In T. Engvall & L. S. Flak (Eds.), *Scientific foundations of digital governance and transformation: Concepts, approaches and challenges* (pp. 25–50). Cham: Springer.

Esposito, M., & Kapoor, A. (2022). *The emerging economies under the dome of the Fourth Industrial Revolution.* Cambridge University Press.

Estevez, E., & Janowski, T. (2013). Leadership and strategies for E-government: Lessons from organizational theory. *Government Information Quarterly, 30*(2), 119–127.

European Institute for Gender Equality. (2020). *Gendered patterns in use of new technologies.* https://eige.europa.eu/publications-resources/toolkits-guides/ gender-equality-index-2020-report/gendered-patterns-use-new-technolo gies?language_content_entity=en.

Eurostat. (n.d.). *Glossary: Digital divide.* https://ec.europa.eu/eurostat/statis tics-explained/index.php?title=Glossary:Digital_divide.

Fomba Kamga, B., Talla Fokam, D. N. D., & Nchofoung, T. N. (2022). Internet access and innovation in developing countries: Some empirical evidence. *Transnational Corporations Review, 15*(3), 1–42.

Fountain, J. E. (2001). *Building the virtual state: Information technology and institutional change.* Brookings Institution Press.

Friedland, R., & Alford, R. R. (1991). Bringing Society Back. In W. W. Powell & P. J. DiMaggio (Eds.), *Symbols, practices, and institutional contradictions. The New Institutionalism in Organizational Analysis* (pp. 76–95). University of Chicago Press.

Green Templeton College. (n.d.). *What are emerging markets?.* University of Oxford.

Grinin, L., Grinin, A., & Korotayev, A. (2022). COVID-19 pandemic as a trigger for the acceleration of the cybernetic revolution, transition from e-government to e-state, and change in social relations. *Technological Forecasting and Social Change, 175*, 121348.

Gupta, A. (2023). Digitalization of the welfare state: Lessons for the emerging economies. *Indian Journal of Public Administration, 69*(2), 453–467. https://doi.org/10.1177/00195561231153903.

Halkias, D., Esposito, M., Harkiolakis, T., Diaz, J., & Ikpogu, N. M. (2023). Digital entrepreneurship and disruptive innovation in the Greek maritime industry: The case of Harbor Lab. In V. Ramadani, S. Kjosev, & B. S. Sergi (Eds.), *Entrepreneurship development in the Balkans: Perspective from diverse contexts* (pp. 131–150). Emerald. https://doi.org/10.1108/978-1-83753-454-820231008.

Hammerschmid, G., Palaric, E., Rackwitz, M., & Wegrich, K. (2023). A shift in paradigm? Collaborative public administration in the context of national digitalization strategies. *Governance*. Advance online publication. https://doi.org/10.1111/gove.12778.

Hartley, J. (2021, November 1). *Indian languages: A useful guide to all the languages spoken in India.* Berlitz. www.berlitz.com/blog/indian-languages-spoken-listhttps://www.oecd.org/dev/Key_Messages_EMnet_WorkingGroup_DigitalTransformation_EmergingMarkets.pdf.

Heeks, R., & Bailur, S. (2007). Analyzing e-government research: Perspectives, philosophies, theories, methods, and practice. *Government Information Quarterly, 24*(2), 243–265.

Leading the Digital Transformation for a Sustainable Future. (2020). Digital Transformation Report 2020. https://dgov.tdra.gov.ae/en/publications/digital-transformation-report.

Henderson, J. V., & Turner, M. A. (2020). Urbanization in the developing world: Too early or too slow? *Journal of Economic Perspectives, 34*(3), 150–173.

Hensmans, M. (2023). Winning the innovation game in emerging markets. *Journal of Business Strategy, 44*(4), 219–227. https://doi.org/10.1108/JBS-03-2022-0042.

Heuberger, M. (2022). *Coordinating digital government: Explaining coordination challenges regarding the digital transformation of public administration in a federal context* [Doctoral dissertation, University of Potsdam]. Publish University Press. https://doi.org/10.25932/publishup-56269.

Horwitz, F., Budhwar, P., & Morley, M. J. (2015). Future trends in human resource management in emerging markets. In F. Horwitz, P. Budhwar, & M. J. Morley (Eds.), *Handbook of human resource management in emerging markets* (pp. 470–488). Edward Elgar.

Hoskisson, R. E., Eden, L., Lau, C. M., & Wright, M. (2000). Strategy in emerging economies. *Academy of Management Journal, 43*(3), 249–267.

Hoskisson, R. E., Wright, M., Filatotchev, I., & Peng, M. W. (2013). Emerging multinationals from mid-range economies: The influence of institutions and factor markets. *Journal of Management Studies, 50*(7), 1295–1321.

Huang, J., & Tsai, K. S. (2022). Securing authoritarian capitalism in the digital age: The political economy of surveillance in China. *The China Journal, 88* (1), 2–28. https://doi.org/10.1086/720144.

IMF. (2021). *International Monetary Fund.* World economic outlook.

Jansen, B., Kadenko, N., Broeders, D., et al. (2023). Pushing boundaries: An empirical view on the digital sovereignty of six governments in the midst of geopolitical tensions. *Government Information Quarterly, 40*(4), 101862.

Kaczorowska, A. (2020). Traditional versus agile project management in public sector in Poland. *Scientific Papers of Silesian University of Technology – Organization and Management Series*, (149), 287–302. http://dx.doi.org/10.29119/1641-3466.2020.149.25.

Karpenko, O., Zaporozhets, T., Tsedik, M., Vasiuk, N., & Osmak, A. (2023). Digital transformations of public administration in countries with transition economies. *European Review, 31*(6), 569–588. https://doi.org/10.1017/S1062798723000522.

Kauma, J. G., Irerib, W. N., & Olweny, N. O. (2022). Challenges facing coherent digitization of government processes across all policy areas and levels of government to enhance efficient public service delivery in Kenya. *Social Sciences & Psychology, 111*(1), 220–228. https://doi.org/10.47119/IJRP10011111020224034.

Khanna, T. (2009). Billions of entrepreneurs: How China and India are reshaping their futures and yours. *Strategic Direction, 25*(10).

Khanna, T., & Palepu, K. (1997). Why focused strategies may be wrong for emerging markets. *Harvard Business Review, 75*(4), 41–51.

Khanna, T., & Palepu, K. G. (2010). *Winning in emerging markets: A road map for strategy and execution.* Harvard Business Press.

Khanna, T., Palepu, K. G., & Sinha, J. (2015). Strategies that fit emerging markets. In *International business strategy* (pp. 615–631). Routledge.

Khanna, T., & Yafeh, Y. (2005). Business groups and risk sharing around the world. *The Journal of Business, 78*(1), 301–340.

Koch, A. H. (2022). Strategic responses of MNCs in emerging markets: Addressing institutional voids associated with informal institutions. *Critical Perspectives on International Business, 18*(2), 137–156. https://doi.org/10.1108/cpoib-12-2019-0099.

Koop, C., & Kessler, P. (2021). Keeping control of regulation? Domestic constraints on the creation of independent authorities in emerging and developing economies. *Governance*, *34*(2), 545–564. https://doi.org/10.1111/gove.12523.

Krishna, B., & Sebastian, M. P. (2021). Examining the relationship between e-government development, nation's cyber-security commitment, business usage and economic prosperity: A cross-country analysis. *Information & Computer Security*, *29*(5), 737–760. https://doi.org/10.1108/ICS-12-2020-0205.

Lemieux, V. L. (2016). One step forward, two steps backward? Does e-government make governments in developing countries more transparent and accountable? https://documents1.worldbank.org/curated/en/966871468196128495/pdf/102962-WP-Box394845B-PUBLIC-WDR16-BP-One-Step-Forward-Lemieux.pdf.

Looks, H. (2022). A reference framework for agile transformation in public administration. In A. Van Looy, B. Weber, & M. Rosemann (Eds.), *Proceedings of the doctoral consortium papers presented at the 34th international conference on advanced information systems engineering* (pp. 62–68). CEUR Workshop Proceedings. https://ceur-ws.org/Vol-3139/paper08.pdf.

Lyngaas, S. (2023). *Millions of Americans' personal data exposed in global hack*. CNN. https://edition.cnn.com/2023/06/16/politics/cyberattack-us-government/index.html.

Lytras, M. D., & Şerban, A. C. (2020). E-government insights to smart cities research: European union (EU) study and the role of regulations. *IEEE Access*, *8*, 65313–65326.

Malamud, O., Cueto, S. Cristia, J., & Beuermann, D. W. (2019). Do children benefit from internet access? Experimental evidence from Peru. *Journal of Development Economics*, *138*, 41–56. https://doi.org/10.1016/j.jdeveco.2018.11.005.

Malik, T. (2022). Digital transformation through the prism of digital identity. *Journal of Public Policy Practitioners*, *1*(2), 33–48. https://doi.org/10.32350/jppp.12.02.

Malodia, S., Dhir, A., Mishra, M., & Bhatti, Z. A. (2021). Future of e-government: An integrated conceptual framework. *Technological Forecasting and Social Change*, *173*, Article 121102. https://doi.org/10.1016/j.techfore.2021.121102.

Markey, D., & Scobell, A. (2023, October 19). *Three things to know about China-India tensions*. United States Institute of Peace. www.usip.org/publications/2023/10/three-things-know-about-china-india-tensions.

Martínez Euklidiadas, M. (2021, April 5). *How digitalization is transforming government in emerging economies*. Tomorrow City. https://tomorrow.city/a/how-digitalization-is-transforming-government-in-emerging-economies.

Maswanganyi, F. T. (2023). Leveraging indigenous languages for efficient local government: An analysis in a South African context. *International Journal of Research in Business and Social Science, 12*(10), 182–190. https://doi.org/10.20525/ijrbs.v12i10.3115.

Matthess, M., & Kunkel, S. (2020). Structural change and digitalization in developing countries: Conceptually linking the two transformations. *Technology in Society, 63*, Article 101428. https://doi.org/10.1016/j.techsoc.2020.101428.

McCoy, J., & Somer, M. (2021). Overcoming polarization. *Journal of Democracy, 32*(1), 6–21. https://doi.org/10.1353/jod.2021.0012.

Mergel, I. (2013). A framework for interpreting social media interactions in the public sector. *Government Information Quarterly, 30*(4), 327–334.

Ministry of Electronics and Information Technology, Government of India, Centre for e-Government, www.meity.gov.in/content/centre-e-governance#:~:text=Centre%20For%20e%2DGovernance%20%7C%20Ministry,Information%20Technology%2C%20Government%20of%20India.

Ministry of the Interior and Safety, National Information Society Agency, www.dgovkorea.go.kr/contact.

Mirkovski, K., Rouibah, K., Lowry, P., Paliszkiewicz, J., & Ganc, M. (2023). Cross-country determinants of citizens' e-government reuse intention: Empirical evidence from Kuwait and Poland. *Information Technology & People*. Advance online publication. https://doi.org/10.1108/ITP-08-2022-0651.

Mishra, S., Alowaidi, M. A., & Sharma, S. K. (2021). Impact of security standards and policies on the credibility of e-government. *Journal of Ambient Intelligence and Humanized Computing*, 1–12. https://link.springer.com/article/10.1007/s12652-020-02767-5.

Moon, M. J. (2002). The evolution of e-government among municipalities: Rhetoric or reality? *Public Administration Review, 62*(4), 424–433.

Mustaf, A., Ibrahim, O., & Mohammed, F. (2020). E-government adoption: A systematic review in the context of developing nations. *International Journal of Innovation: IJI Journal, 8*(1), 59–76. http://dx.doi.org/10.5585/iji.v8i1.343.

Mynenko, S., & Lyulyov, O. (2022). The impact of digitalization on the transparency of public authorities. *Business Ethics and Leadership, 6*(2), 103–115. https://doi.org/10.21272/bel.6(2).103-115.2022.

National E-Government Division. (n.d.). *UMANG*. Government of India. https://negd.gov.in/umang/.

Observatory of Public Sector Innovation. (n.d.). *Digital transformation*. https://oecd-opsi.org/guide/digital-transformation/.

O'Donnell M., & Turner M. (2013). Leading the world: Public sector reform and e-government in Korea. *The Economic and Labour Relations Review, 24* (4), 533–548. https://doi.org/10.1177/1035304613508870, www.cambridge .org/core/journals/the-economic-and-labour-relations-review/article/abs/ leading-the-world-public-sector-reform-and-egovernment-in-korea/ 1CAE74C5448CB138564339E2F96AE8F2.

Onsongo, E. (2023). Frugal innovation in public service delivery: Reflections from case studies in Kenya. In A. Leliveld, S. Bhaduri, P. Knorringa, & C. van Beers (Eds.), *Handbook on frugal innovation* (pp. 364–378). Edward Elgar. https://doi.org/10.4337/9781788118873.00034.

Organisation for Economic Co-operation and Development. (2019). *Regulatory effectiveness in the era of digitalization.* www.oecd.org/gov/regulatory-policy/Regulatory-effectiveness-in-the-era-of-digitalisation.pdf.

Organization for Economic Co-operation and Development. (2021). *The e-leaders handbook on the governance of digital government.* https://doi .org/10.1787/ac7f2531-en.

Organization for Economic Co-operation and Development. (2023). *Digital government review of Latin America and the Caribbean.* https://doi.org/10 .1787/29f32e64-en.

Padden, M. (2023). The transformation of surveillance in the digitalisation discourse of the OECD: A brief genealogy. *Internet Policy Review, 12*(3), 1–39. http://hdl.handle.net/10419/278803.

Paksi, A., Yoon, S., Anand, P., & Lee, K. (2022). Let local voices be heard: A tale of partnership for e-Government. *Development in Practice, 32*(6), 793–803.

Pamungkas, S. H. A., Prasetyo, K., & Walinegoro, B. G. (2023). Public security vs personal privacy: Analysis of PeduliLindungi from open government and surveillance state perspectives. *KnE Social Sciences*, 601–623. https://kneo pen.com/KnE-Social/article/view/13026/.

Paul, M., Upadhyay, P., & Dwivedi, Y. K. (2020). Roadmap to digitalisation of an emerging economy: A viewpoint. *Transforming Government: People, Process and Policy, 14*(3), 401–415.

Penfold, M. (2018). *Food, technology, and authoritarianism in Venezuela's elections.* Wilson Center. www.wilsoncenter.org/sites/default/files/media/ documents/misc/penfold_venezuela_elections_final.pdf.

Petlach, M. (2023). Digitalization of public diplomacy: An instance of nation branding and its use in Southeast Asia. In M. Petlach (Ed.), *Global perspectives on the emerging trends in public diplomacy* (pp. 75–101). IGI Global.

PIB Delhi. (2023, January 31). *Economic survey highlights thrust on rural development* [Press release]. Ministry of Finance, Government of India. https://pib.gov.in/PressReleasePage.aspx?PRID=1894901.

Plummer, R. (2015). Giving everyone in the world an address. *BBC News* (Online Edition) April 30, 2015. www.bbc.com/news/business-32444811.

Pomaza-Ponomarenko, A. L., Hren, L. M., Durman, O. L., Bondarchuk, N. V., & Vorobets, V. (2020). Management mechanisms in the context of digitization of all spheres of society. *Revista San Gregorio, 1*(42), 1–9. https://revista.sangregorio.edu.ec/index.php/REVISTASANGREGORIO/article/view/1535.

Radjou, N., & Prabhu, J. (2012). Mobilizing for growth in emerging markets. *MIT Sloan Management Review.*

Ranchordás, S. (2022). The digitization of government and digital exclusion: Setting the scene. University of Groningen Faculty of Law Research Paper No. 30/2020. *The Rule of Law in Cyberspace,* 125–148. http://dx.doi.org/10.2139/ssrn.3663051.

Rehman, K., Shah, A. A., & Ahmed, K. (2018). E-Government identification to accomplish sustainable development goals (UN 2030 Agenda) a case study of Pakistan. In K. Rehman, A. A. Shah, & K. Ahmed (Eds.), *2018 IEEE global humanitarian technology conference (GHTC)* (pp. 1-6). Institute of Electrical and Electronics Engineers. https://doi.org/10.1109/GHTC.2018.8601890.

Rendon, M., & Kohan, A. (2019, December 4). *The internet: Venezuela's lifeline.* Center for Strategic and International Studies. www.csis.org/analysis/internet-venezuelas-lifeline.

Resecurity. (2023, October 15). *PII belonging to Indian citizens, including their Aadhaar IDs, offered for sale on the dark web.* www.resecurity.com/blog/article/pii-belonging-to-indian-citizens-including-their-aadhaar-ids-offered-for-sale-on-the-dark-web.

Rossidis, I., Mihiotis, A., & Ntalakos, A. (2023). The contribution of change management to the integration of e-governance systems. In D. Belias, I. Rossidis, C. Papademetriou, A. Masouras, & S. Anastasiadou (Eds.), *Managing successful and ethical organizational change* (pp. 196–216). IGI Global. https://doi.org/10.4018/979-8-3693-0235-4.ch009.

Rottig, D. (2016). Institutions and emerging markets: Effects and implications for multinational corporations. *International Journal of Emerging Markets, 11*(1), 2–17.

Rottig, D., & de Oliveira, R. T. (2019). International expansion of Chinese emerging market multinational corporations to developed markets: A qualitative analysis of post-acquisition and integration strategies. *Chinese acquisitions in developed countries: Operational challenges and opportunities* (pp. 37–53). Springer.

Rutashobya, L. K., Chiwona-Karltun, L., Wilson, M., Ilomo, M., & Semkunde, M. (2021). Gender and rural entrepreneurship in digitizing sub-Saharan Africa. In J. B. Abugre, E. L. C. Osabutey, & S. P. Sigué (Eds.), *Business in Africa in the era of digital technology: Essays in honour of Professor William Darley* (pp. 63–84). Springer Cham. https://doi.org/10.1007/978-3-030-70538-1_5.

Sadik-Zada, E. R., Gatto, A., & Niftiyev, I. (2022). E-government and petty corruption in public sector service delivery. *Technology Analysis & Strategic Management.* Advance online publication. https://doi.org/10.1080/09537325.2022.2067037.

Sabharwal, S., & Sharma, S. (2020). Ransomware attack: India issues red alert. In J. K. Mandal & D. Bhattacharya (Eds.), *Emerging technology in modelling and graphics: Proceedings of IEM graph 2018* (pp. 471–484). Springer Singapore. https://doi.org/10.1007/978-981-13-7403-6_42.

Samuel, M., Doctor, G., Christian, P., & Baradi, M. (2020). Drivers and barriers to e-government adoption in Indian cities. *Journal of Urban Management, 9* (4), 408-417. https://doi.org/10.1016/j.jum.2020.05.002.

Satoglu, E. B. (2020). FDI into emerging markets: Do institutions really matter? *International Journal of Research in Business and Social Science (2147–4478), 9*(5), 200–211. https://doi.org/10.20525/ijrbs.v9i5.867.

Schlogl, L., & Kim, K. (2023). After authoritarian technocracy: The space for industrial policy-making in democratic developing countries. *Third World Quarterly, 44*(9), 1938–1959. https://doi.org/10.1080/01436597.2021.1984876.

Shah, I. A., Wassan, S., & Usmani, M. H. (2022). E-Government security and privacy issues: Challenges and preventive approaches. *Cybersecurity Measures for E-Government Frameworks* (pp. 61–76). https://www.igi-global.com/chapter/e-government-security-and-privacy-issues/302721.

Sharma, A. (2018, July 29). No data has been fetched using RS Sharma's Aadhaar number: Government. *The Economic Times.* https://economictimes.indiatimes.com/news/politics-and-nation/no-data-has-been-fetched-using-rs-sharmas-aadhaar-number-government/articleshow/65184621.cms.

Singh, P. (2021). Aadhaar and data privacy: Biometric identification and anxieties of recognition in India. *Information, Communication & Society, 24*(7), 978–993. https://doi.org/10.1080/1369118X.2019.1668459.

Siqueira, M. S., Dias, F. S., Rigatto, S. H., et al. (2023). Who watches the watchers? Accessibility of the public prosecutor's office websites in Brazil and implications for e-government accessibility surveillance policies. *Electronic Government, an International Journal, 19*(1), 72–94.

Thathoo, C. (2022, July 20). *UIDAI invites top hackers to expose vulnerabilities in Aadhaar's security system.* Inc42. https://inc42.com/buzz/uidai-invites-20-top-hackers-to-figure-out-vulnerabilities-in-aadhaars-security-system/.

Trischler, J., & Westman Trischler, J. (2022). Design for experience – a public service design approach in the age of digitalization. *Public Management Review, 24*(8), 1251–1270. https://doi.org/10.1080/14719037.2021.1899272.

Tse, T., Esposito, M., & Goh, D. (2023). AI-powered ESG: Our chance to make a real difference?. In *The digital transformation playbook: What you need to know and do* (2nd ed., pp. 166–175). Project Management Institute.

The United Arab Emirates' Government Portal, Digital UAE, https://u.ae/en/about-the-uae/digital-uae.

United Nations Department of Economic and Social Affairs. (2022). *UN e-government survey 2022.* https://publicadministration.un.org/egovkb/en-us/Reports/UN-E-Government-Survey-2022.

United Nations Division for Public Institutions and Digital Government. (n.d.). *Overview.* United Nations. Retrieved November 10, 2023, from https://publicadministration.un.org/egovkb/en-us/Overview.

Upadhyay, P., Kumar, A., Dwivedi, Y. K., & Adlakha, A. (2022). Continual usage intention of platform-based governance services: A study from an emerging economy. *Government Information Quarterly, 39*(1), 101651.

Uruguay's Digital Policy, https://govtech.uy/uruguays-digital-policy/.

Valle-Cruz, D. (2019). Public value of e-government services through emerging technologies. *International Journal of Public Sector Management, 32*(5), 530–545.

Valle-Cruz, D., & García-Contreras, R. (2023). Towards AI-driven transformation and smart data management: Emerging technological change in the public sector value chain. *Public Policy and Administration.* Advance online publication. https://doi.org/10.1177/09520767231188401.

Vidal, L. (2018, December 17). *Venezuelans shudder at news of biometric ID deal with Chinese tech giant.* Global Voices. https://globalvoices.org/2018/12/27/venezuelans-shudder-at-news-of-biometric-id-deal-with-chinese-tech-giant/.

Vidal, L. (2018, December 28). *Venezuelans fear "Fatherland Card" may be a new form of social control.* The World. https://theworld.org/stories/2018-12-28/venezuelans-fear-fatherland-card-may-be-new-form-social-control.

Vîlceanu, D. M. (2022, June). E-government in Public Services. In D. M. Vilceanu (Ed.), *Proceedings of the 28th international RAIS conference on social sciences and humanities* (pp. 72–77). Scientia Moralitas Research Institute.

Vyas-Doorgapersad, S. (2022). The use of digitalization (ICTs) in achieving sustainable development goals. *Global Journal of Emerging Market Economies*, *14*(2), 265–278. https://doi.org/10.1177/09749101211067295.

Wandaogo, A. A. (2022). Does digitalization improve government effectiveness? Evidence from developing and developed countries. *Applied Economics*, *54* (33), 3840–3860. https://doi.org/10.1080/00036846.2021.2016590.

Welter, F., & Smallbone, D. (2011). Institutional perspectives on entrepreneurial behavior in challenging environments. *Journal of Small Business Management*, *49*(1), 107–125.

World Economic Forum & FTI Consulting. (2023). *Digital transition framework: An action plan for public-private collaboration* [White Paper]. https://www3.weforum.org/docs/WEF_Digital_Transition_Framework_2023.pdf.

Wouters, S., Janssen, M., Lember, V., & Crompvoets, J. (2023). Strategies to advance the dream of integrated digital public service delivery in inter-organizational collaboration networks. *Government Information Quarterly*, *40*(1), Article 101779. https://doi.org/10.1016/j.giq.2022.101779.

Xu, X., Kostka, G., & Cao, X. (2022). Information control and public support for social credit systems in China. *The Journal of Politics*, *84*(4), 2230–2245. https://doi.org/10.1086/718358.

Yapur, N., & Vasquez, A. (2021, April 14). *Venezuela politicizes vaccine access via state loyalty card*. Bloomberg. www.bloomberg.com/news/articles/2021-04-14/venezuela-politicizes-access-to-vaccines-via-state-loyalty-card.

Yeniceler, İ., & Ilgın, H. Ö. (2019, April). New media and digital surveillance reflections. In *Proceedings of the Communication and Technology Congress, Online* (Vol. 17).

Yavwa, Y., & Twinomurinzi, H. (2021). Intricacy of indigenous culture on digital government adoption: A systematic review. *International Journal of Technology, Knowledge and Society*, *17*(1), 49–68. https://doi.org/10.18848/1832-3669/CGP/v17i01/49-68.

Yildirim, A., Clarysse, B., & Wright, M. (2022). The impact of institutional voids and ecosystem logics in the spread of ecosystems in emerging economies. *Industry and Innovation*, *29*(5), 649–671. https://doi.org/10.1080/13662716.2021.2007760.

Cambridge Elements ᐥ

Economics of Emerging Markets

Bruno S. Sergi

Harvard University

Editor Bruno S. Sergi is an Instructor at Harvard University, an Associate of the Harvard University Davis Center for Russian and Eurasian Studies and Harvard University Asia Center. He is the Academic Series Editor of the Cambridge *Elements in the Economics of Emerging Markets* (Cambridge University Press), a co-editor of the *Lab for Entrepreneurship and Development* book series, and associate editor of *The American Economist*. Concurrently, he teaches International Political Economics at the University of Messina, Scientific Director of the Lab for Entrepreneurship and Development (LEAD), and a co-founder and Scientific Director of the International Center for Emerging Markets Research at RUDN University in Moscow. He has published over 200 articles in professional journals and twenty-one books as author, co-author, editor, and co-editor.

About the Series

The aim of this Elements series is to deliver state-of-the-art, comprehensive coverage of the knowledge developed to date, including the dynamics and prospects of these economies, focusing on emerging markets' economics, finance, banking, technology advances, trade, demographic challenges, and their economic relations with the rest of the world, as well as the causal factors and limits of economic policy in these markets.

Cambridge Elements ⹀

Economics of Emerging Markets

Printed in the United States
by Baker & Taylor Publisher Services